E. Mansione - L. Pazie

ROME

FROM ANTIQUITY TO THE PRESENT DAY

Scala, Firenze

CONTENTS

© COPYRIGHT 1981 by SCALA Istituto Fotografico Editoriale,
Via Chiantigiana 62 50011 Antella (Firenze)
Photographs: SCALA Firenze and ARCA Roma
Produced by SCALA Istituto Fotografico Editoriale
Printed in Italy by SAGDOS Brugherio 1981

ISBN 0-935748-37-7 U.S.A. Pbk.
ISBN 0-584-95004-7 U.K. Pbk.

Cover: View of the Roman Forum looking towards the rostra and the Temple of Saturn.

Back-cover: Vatican City, view of the Fountain of the Sacrament and the dome of St Peter's.

Inside front and back-cover:
Ignazio Danti (1536-86), Map of Rome. Vatican Museums, Gallery of Maps.
Giovan Battista Piranesi (1720-78), Map of Rome and the Campus Martius, from his book of engravings « Monumenti di Roma » dedicated to Clement XIV.

INTRODUCTION

No visitor to the Eternal City can fail to be overwhelmed by the sheer range and completeness of its attractions. Rome has always played a major part in the history of the world, and on every side we confront ruined temples, noble churches, stately palaces, and spectacular fountains that fill us with reverence. The proud title *Roma Caput Mundi* (Rome, head of the world) is no idle boast. Every century of its history is recorded by outstanding monuments in a great variety of styles. The lover of art is offered an unrivalled breadth of choice, an overwhelming panoply of riches. The ruined temples and statues of the ancients, the basilicas and mosaics of the Early Christian period, the perfection and splendour of the Renaissance, the exuberance and eccentricity of the Baroque are all to be found here in dazzling profusion. Rome is one vast monument to artistic beauty, the grandest and most ceaselessly fascinating work of art of all.

Even the less artistically inclined will find themselves inspired by the atmosphere of this unique city. It lives among the columns and the ruins of the Roman Empire, it cascades through the waters of the fountains, it dwells in the noble palaces, and goes straight to the heart. We are all, of whatever nation or creed, heirs to this profusion of all that we value and mean by the word civilisation.

Legend relates that Rea Silvia, a Vestal Virgin descended from Aeneas through her father King of the Latins, was ravished by the god Mars, and forced to break her vow of chastity. The result of her misfortune was the birth of twins, who were abandoned in a basket cast into the River Tiber. When

1. THE CAPITOLINE WOLF (Etruscan bronze, 6th century BC, Palazzo dei Conservatori). The wolf suckling the twins Romulus and Remus, the founders of Rome, has remained the symbol of the city.

the basket miraculously came to rest on the bank, the new-born children cried out in their hunger, and were suckled by a she-wolf who heard them. A shepherd called Faustulus found the twins and he and his wife took care of them and named them Romulus and Remus. They grew up strong and bold, and the discovery of their father's divinity made them determine to found a city. They selected a site near the Tiber, between seven hills, and traced the boundaries of the city on the ground. An argument arose about whose name the city should be given, and Romulus killed Remus.

This then is the legend of the foundation of Rome, which is supposed to have taken place on April 21st, 753 BC. With its central position in the peninsula and its proximity to the sea, the city soon became a major trading centre for the surrounding area. During the rule of the Seven Kings of Rome the Romans waged war on the neighbouring tribes and increased their domain. The city attracted people form the surrounding regions, and grew in size until it covered the seven hills: the Palatine, Capitoline, Aventine, Esquiline, Viminal, Quirinal, and Caelian.

In 510 BC Rome became a Republic. It was razed to the ground by the Gauls in 387 BC and severely defeated by Hannibal's Carthaginian army in the Second Punic War (218-201 BC); but later Rome occupied Spain, and finally overcame its Carthaginian rival in 146 BC. Soon Rome dominated the whole Italian peninsula and had conquered Greece and much of the Mediterranean world. Between 58 and 49 BC Julius Caesar campaigned in Gaul, invading Britain in 54 BC. But civil unrest and fighting between various factions led to Caesar's murder in 44 BC, and eventually to the founding of the Roman Empire by Augustus in 27 BC, which marked the end of the republic and of the rule of the Senate.

This was also the great age of Roman literature: Cicero (106-44 BC) left many speeches and letters which give some idea of the life of the governing class at the time; Virgil (70-19 BC wrote his great epic poem the *Aeneid* concerning the legendary founding of Rome by the Trojan Aeneas; Horace (65-8 BC) composed odes; Livy (59 BC-17 AD), a history of Rome; and Ovid (43 BC-18 AD) created a romantic and fabulous world in his *Metamorphoses*.

The city itself was magnificent: during the rule of the Emperor Augustus (27 BC-14 AD) it could boast 11 aqueducts, 8 bridges over the Tiber, 1000 private bathing places, 11 forums, 1152 fountains, 28 libraries, 2 circuses, 3 theatres, and 2 *naumachia* (arenas where naval battles were staged on artificial lakes).

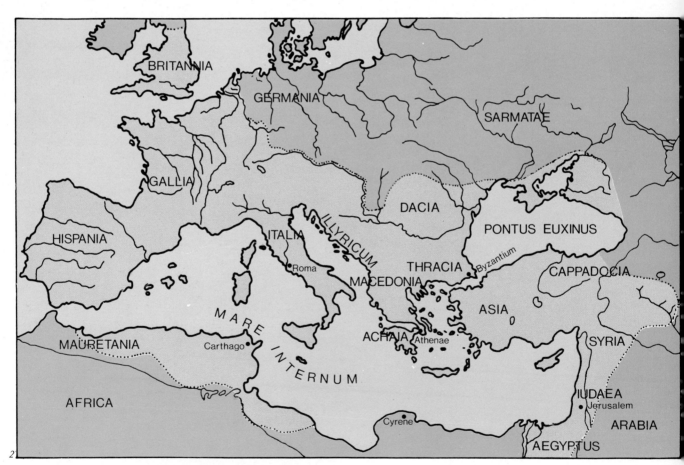

2. MAP OF THE ROMAN EMPIRE C. 230 AD showing the extent of the Roman domination of the Mediterranean, North Africa and almost all of Europe.

By the end of the 2nd century AD Rome, by means of wars, alliances, and campaigns, had increased in power until its Mediterranean-based Empire extended to the Danube, to Macedonia, Syria, Armenia, Mesopotamia, Germany, and Britain. All these territories reaped the benefits of Rome's remarkable culture and enlightened legal system, while at the centre of the Empire the city grew so large that it could accommodate a population of one and a half million. The state and the ruling classes became immensely rich, and life was spent between banquets, festivals, and sophisticated debaucheries. Physical exercise and the arts of war fell into decline. The decadence of Rome's emperors and the lack of military power aided the invasion of Alaric and his Goths (408 AD), and Rome was sacked in 410, 455, and 472. The Empire disintegrated, and the population of the city itself fell below 100,000.

But, in the meantime, after many years of persecution, the tolerance of Christianity had been proclaimed in 313 AD by Constantine the Great in the Edict of Milan. As this religion spread throughout Europe, once again Rome became a vital centre, this time for millions of pilgrims and penitents. Using the precious marbles and metals of the temples and palaces of Ancient Rome, the popes made Rome great again. It was at this time that the great early Christian basilicas were constructed: Old St Peter's (according to legend on the site of St Peter's grave), Santa Maria Maggiore, St John Lateran, and Santa Cecilia. Throughout this time the papal residence was at the Lateran. But Rome was not free from trouble: territorial disputes between the papacy and the Holy Roman Emperor in the 12th century led to strife throughout the peninsula; in 1309 the papal court moved to Avignon where it stayed until 1411. During che Great Schism (1378-1417), French and Italian rival candidates vied for supremacy.

Only in the 15th century did the papacy return to Rome; Martin V (1417-21), a Roman by birth, began to rebuild the ancient city. The ncxt hundred years saw it transformed: new roads were constructed, churches, palaces, and hospitals were built, and finally in 1506 the rebuilding of St Peter's began. Once again, it became the artistic capital of Europe, and during the Renaissance and Baroque periods it attracted all the greatest artists of the day: Bramante, Sangallo, Raphael, Michelangelo, Vignola, Maderno, Bernini, and Borromini all created immortal works in Rome.

The rule of the popes lasted until 1870, the year in which Rome was annexed to the new-born Kingdom of Italy and proclaimed its capital.

3

3. BATTLE BETWEEN ROMANS AND BARBARIANS (Roman sarcophagus, 3rd century AD, Museo delle Terme). The victorious general is either Volusian or Claudius II.

4. MODEL OF THE CITY OF ROME IN THE 4TH CENTURY AD (Museum of Roman Civilisation). In the foreground is the Circus Maximus, in the middle distance on the right is the Colosseum and to its left the Roman Forum.

THE ROMAN FORUM

The word 'Forum', etymologically obscure, was used by the Ancients to describe that part of the city which was the meeting-place and topographical centre where political, administrative and commercial activity was based. Rome had its Forum in the valley situated between the hills overlooking the Tiber, from which it was possible to control all the surrounding region. Although the area was marshy and unhealthy, it was chosen by the founders of the city because the Tiber, as well as being the only link between the Mediterranean and the Appennines, represented an ideal point of contact for the peoples of Upper Lazio and Campania.

In the early years after the foundation of Rome there was no building activity in the valley of the Forum apart from a few archaic tombs, on account of the site's susceptibility to flooding. But as the population and the importance of the city increased, it became vitally necessary to create a meeting-place that could be used all the year round. The construction of the *Cloaca Maxima*, a great underground sewer over half a mile long, during the reign of Tarquinius Priscus (6th century BC) drained the water from the marsh and channelled it off into the Tiber, thus rendering the valley habitable.

Once this heroic task had been effected, construction began on the temples, the basilicas, the Senate, and on the commemorative monuments that recorded the victories and conquests that made Rome the centre of the world. To name them all, given that they span so many centuries of history, would be an impossible task in as short a space as is available here.

Let us instead begin by taking the **Arch of Septimius Severus** (north end of the Forum) and make it our point of departure from which to see the most important monuments. This large triumphal arch was erected at the start of the 3rd century AD to commemorate the victory of the Roman army over the Parthians of ancient Persia. Its historical interest resides in the fact that it is among the first arches built to celebrate, not a conquest, but a war waged to put down an inva-

5

5, 6. IMAGINARY RECONSTRUCTION OF THE ROMAN FORUM IN THE 4TH CENTURY AD. Temples, basilicas and triumphal arches are interspersed with columns celebrating victories, and statues of generals and orators.

sion of the Empire; it ushers in the period of Roman decadence after centuries of expansion. Immediately beside it are the remains of the *rostra*, the official platforms from which orators declaimed their speeches to the assembled populace. Only a part of the marble stair and of the platform's supporting masonry are still visible. The bronze *rostra*, or « beaks », from the prows of captured ships, which once decorated the front of the edifice and from which the place took its name, have long since disappeared. The most eye-catching monument in this part of the Forum is the imposing **Temple of Saturn**, of which the entire base and eight large Ionic columns of rose granite remain intact. This temple, which is one of the oldest surviving in Rome, was built towards the end of the period of the Kings (6th-5th centuries BC), at about the same period as the Temple of Jupiter on the Capitol. It was the depository of the Public Treasury (*Aerarium Publicum*). The present structure dates from the Imperial period (2nd century AD) when the temple was reconstructed after a fire, a fact recorded in an inscription on the frieze.

To its right, below the slope of the Capitoline Hill, are the remains of three temples. From left to right they are: **The Portico of the Dii Consentes**, built under the Emperor Julian the Apostate in the 4th century, one of the last pagan monuments during the Christian era; **The Temple of Vespasian**, of which there remain three superb columns, and which was dedicated to the deified Emperor by the Senate. It marks the beginning of the reconstruction of the city after the terrible fire of Nero (64 AD); **The Temple of Concord**, of which

lica Julia: we can still see the bases of the four rows of columns. This building, which served as a court and as a covered meeting-place, was begun in 54 BC by order of Julius Caesar to replace the Basilica Sempronia; it was destroyed by fire many times but always rebuilt. We next come to one of the most important and majestic buildings of Imperial Rome, just the other side of the Vicus Tuscus, the **Temple of Castor and Pollux**. According to legend, the two demi-gods appeared at this spot to announce the victory at the Battle of Lake Regillus, at which the Romans succeeded in expelling the ruling Tarquin family (496 BC). The Temple was constructed here to record this significant event, which in political terms marked a crucial moment of change in the system of government of Ancient Rome. Indeed, with the passing of absolute monarchy, the Greek system of democracy was adopted, although the Romans gave it a more pragmatic flavour. Citizens of every social class had their part to play in the life of the city. The motto S.P.Q.R., *Senatus PopulusQue Romanus* (the Senate and the People of Rome), expresses just this idea.

Beyond the Temple of Castor and Pollux is the **Temple of Vesta** and the remains of the **House of the Vestal Virgins**, the round temple contained the Holy Fire, kept ever burning by the Vestals, and symbolising the unquenchable fire of Love for Family and Country. To the left of the Temple of Vesta are the remains of the **Temple of Julius Caesar**, at the centre of which Caesar's ashes were placed after his cremation. It is also the place where Mark Anthony made his famous speech in honour of Caesar. From a historical point of

6

only the podium survives, built in 367 BC to celebrate the peace between patricians and plebeians achieved through the Licinean Law, which gave the two social classes political equality. At the rear of these three temples are the remains of the **Tabularium**, which was the State Archive (1st century BC).

To the left of the Temple of Saturn was the rectangular **Basi-**

view the great importance of the temple derives from the fact that, with the Senate's permission, the Emperor Augustus succeeded in establishing the principle of the Emperor's divinity, and of his total power both temporal and spiritual. The establishment of this tenet of belief was one of the fundamental reasons for the Emperors' opposition to Christianity which led to the persecution of its adherants.

7

8

7. THE ROMAN FORUM
VIEWED FROM THE WEST. *The
foreground is dominated by the remains of
the Tabularium, behind which, on the left
is the Arch of Septimius Severus; the
Sacra Via ran straight through the
Forum to the Arch of Titus, visible in the
distance.*

8. MODEL OF THE ROMAN
FORUM IN THE 4TH CENTURY
AD (Museum of Roman Civilisation):
  1. *Temple of Concord*
  2. *Tabularium (State Archives)*
  3. *Temple of Saturn*
  4. *Basilica Julia*
  5. *Temple of Castor and Pollux*
  6. *Temple of Julius Caesar*
  7. *Temple of Vesta*
  8. *Temple of Venus and Rome*
  9. *Basilica of Maxentius*
  10. *Temple of Antoninus and Faustina*
  11. *Basilica Emilia*
  12. *The Curia (seat of the Senate)*
  13. *Forum of Peace or of Vespasian*
  14. *Forum Transitorium*
  15. *Forum of Julius Caesar*
  16. *Imperial Palaces on the Palatine*

9. THE HOUSE OF THE
VESTAL VIRGINS. *Consisting of a
central courtyard, around which stood the
dwellings of the Vestals.*

9

10. MODEL OF THE BASILICA
OF MAXENTIUS (*Museum of
Roman Civilisation*).

10

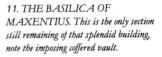

11. THE BASILICA OF
MAXENTIUS. *This is the only section
still remaining of that splendid building,
note the imposing coffered vault.*

11

12

13

Further on, as if to mark the centre of Rome and of the whole world, stands the **Arch of Titus**. This was built after the conquest and destruction of Jerusalem (70 AD), and its interior is decorated with reliefs representing the *Triumph of Titus* and the *Transportation to Rome of the Seven-branched Candlestick from the Temple of Jerusalem*. To the left of the Temple of Caesar, almost at the centre of the Forum, is the fine and well preserved **Temple of Antoninus and Faustina** (2nd century AD), which has been converted into the church of San Lorenzo in Miranda and endowed with a Baroque facade. Clearly visible to its side are the rectangular plan and remaining columns of the **Basilica Emilia**, the only republican basilica of which any trace survives. It was begun in 170 BC, by order of the Censors Emilius Lepidus and Fulvius Nobilior. The area immediately in front of the basilica was always left open and served as a meeting-place. Here orators declaimed speeches, official judgements were announced, merchants and farmers sold their wares. Public executions and funerals were also held here. Through this area runs the **Sacra Via**, the oldest street of Rome. Originally it was lined with shrines. When a victorious general was granted a triumph, it was down this road that he drove, in a chariot surrounded by his trophies, his

12. THE TEMPLE OF VESTA. This circular temple housed the eternal fire, sacred to Vesta, goddess of the hearth, which was guarded by the Vestal Virgins. It was rebuilt repeatedly, lastly by Septimius Severus in 191 AD.

13. THE TEMPLE OF CASTOR AND POLLUX. Originally built in the 5th century BC, it was reconstructed many times. The twin gods, Castor and Pollux, were the patrons of Roman knights.

14. THE ARCH OF TITUS. *Situated on the summit of the Sacra Via, this arch was erected in memory of the Emperor Titus after his death in 81 AD. The reliefs inside the arch depict his triumphal procession.*

15. THE TRIUMPH OF TITUS *(freize from the Arch of Titus). The soldiers in procession carry the seven-branched candlestick from the temple of Jerusalem.*

16

16. VIEW OF THE ROMAN FORUM. In the foreground the three Corinthian columns of the Temple of Castor and Pollux and in the background the Arch of Septimius Severus.

soldiers and his prisoners, to offer sacrifice at the Temple of Jupiter.

Finally, beside the Arch of Septimius Severus, stands the **Curia**, the seat of the Senate. Its name, *Curia Julia*, records the fact that it was started by Julius Caesar to replace the *Curia Hostilia*, which was destroyed by fire in 52 BC. Many times restored, especially at the time of Diocletian (3rd century AD), it has re-

mained perfectly preserved, because it was converted into a church in the 7th century. Over the centuries the social and political life of Ancient Rome was governed by the laws that were debated and passed in this building. It has not been possible to discuss every building and monument in the Forum, but the overall impression gained here more than anywhere else is that we are truly at the heart of the Ancient World.

THE PALATINE

The Palatine Hill, surrounded by the other hills of Rome and very close to the Tiber, was an ideal place for a nomadic tribe to settle because of its gentle slopes and its position in relation to the river. In addition, the Palatine occupied a commanding strategic position, naturally protected by the Tiber Island and dominating the two routes that connected the Etruscan region with Campania. The spot was securely protected by the natural fortresses of the Aventine and the Capitol, and it was here that the original city of Rome was founded. Indeed, recent archaeological excavation has confirmed the antiquity of the site.

During the period of the Republic, the Palatine was one of the most elegant and sumptuous areas of the city. It was inhabited by the most important figures of Rome: here were the villas and houses of men such as Cicero. At the start of the Imperial era, after the Battle of Actium, Augustus, who had been born on the Palatine, decided to transfer his residence to this seat of the ancient kings. Over the following centuries other lavish buildings erected here by the Emperors Tiberius, Caligula, and Septimius Severus, transformed the character of the hill. It became a majestic private complex of buildings in which the emperors lived, and from which they governed all the known world.

17

18

17. REMAINS OF BUILDINGS OF THE IMPERIAL ERA ON THE PALATINE. Originally the site of the earliest settlement of the Latin tribe, it became the most exclusive area of the city in the Imperial era.

18. MODEL OF THE PALATINE (Museum of Roman Civilisation).

THE IMPERIAL FORUMS

As Rome grew in political importance in the Mediterranean, the small city built among the seven hills became the centre of a political, commercial, and economic empire. By the end of the Republic (1st century BC) many people had moved into the metropolis, and the administrators had to cope with a population explosion. In addition to enlarging Rome beyond the old city walls, all available space near the Forum was utilized to improve the organization of the city.

By the time of Julius Caesar the population of Rome had reached one million inhabitants, and he decided to enlarge the Forum; this expansion was continued by his successors, thereby creating a new urban centre, the group of buildings now known as the Imperial Forums. The **Forum of Caesar**, begun by Julius Caesar, was completed by Augustus, who himself built a second forum. A third was built by Vespasian around the Temple of Peace, and a fourth, the **Forum Transitorium**, was begun by Domitian and completed by Nerva. The last to be built was **Trajan's Forum**.

19. TRAJAN'S COLUMN (Trajan's Forum). Dedicated to the Emperor in 113 AD to commemorate his victory over the Dacians; the spiral relief depicts his campaigns. Originally crowned with Trajan's statue it was replaced by that of St Peter.

20. TRAJAN'S FORUM. The last and most splendid of the Imperial Forums to be built, it was constructed by the Emperor Trajan (98-117 AD). The semi-circular building is Trajan's Market.

19

THE CIRCUS MAXIMUS

The valley between the Aventine and Palatine hills was always an important meeting-place. Very probably fairs and markets were held here and, given the long, flat expanse of land, it is likely that chariot and horse races were organized on holidays. King Tarquinius Priscus is credited with building the first hippodrome on the site, a comparatively small wooden structure. This was replaced by a solid walled construction, parts of which date from the 4th century BC. It was probably at this time that the *spina*, a long wall running along the centre, was built. The water that ran from the hills down to the Tiber was channelled under it. Additions and improvements were made over the centuries: in 174 BC seven large marble eggs were placed on the **spina** to act as lap-counters, and later the Obelisk of Rameses II, which had been brought from Heliopolis, was placed at its centre. (The obelisk is now in Piazza del Popolo). By the time of Augustus, the Circus Maximus had reached its maximum size, measuring 621 metres in length with a seating capacity of just over 150,000.

Later it was restored and reconstructed many times: by Caligula, Claudius, Nero (after the fire of 64 AD), and lastly by Trajan, when its capacity was increased to over 250,000. Constant II added a second obelisk to the *spina*. It came from Thebes, where it was dedicated to Thutmosis II and III (15th century BC), and is the tallest (32.50 metres) and oldest obelisk to have been brought to Rome in antiquity. It now stands in the square of St John Lateran, where it was transferred by Pope Sixtus V.

The circus was used throughout the year for two and four-horse chariot races, culminating in the first half of September with the Roman Games. The Circus Maximus may also have been used for other spectacles, such as triumphs. Only part of the structure has been excavated: a section on the south side, where a triumphal arch, dedicated to Titus and Vespasian, was built to commemorate the conquest of Palestine and serve as a monumental entrance.

21

21. MODEL OF THE CIRCUS MAXIMUS (Museum of Roman Civilisation).
Originally made of wood, it was subsequently enlarged to hold 250,000 spectators.
Chariot races and triumphal processions were held here.

THE ARCH OF CONSTANTINE

The Arch of Constantine is the best preserved triumphal arch in Rome. It was built to commemorate the victory of the Emperor Constantine over Maxentius at the Battle of the Milvian Bridge on October 28th, 312 AD. It was completed about three years later using columns, statues, and reliefs taken from other buildings of various periods. The Trajanic bas-reliefs above and the Hadrianic circular scenes of hunting lower down are particularly impressive.

22. THE ARCH OF CONSTANTINE. Detail of the attic with statues of barbarians, and reliefs depicting the wars of Marcus Aurelius.

23. THE ARCH OF CONSTANTINE. Built to commemorate the Emperor's victory at the Milvian Bridge in 312 AD, it was constructed of reliefs and columns taken from earlier buildings.

22

23

THE COLOSSEUM

The Romans called this imposing edifice the Flavian Amphitheatre, because the Emperor Vespasian, who began it in 72 AD, and his son, the Emperor Titus, who completed it only eight years later in 80 AD, were both members of the Flavian dynasty. At the time of its construction the population of Rome was increasing rapidly; one amphitheatre (that of Taurus) had been damaged by fire, and two others were merely temporary constructions. Consequently the new Flavian dynasty made the shrewd decision to build a vast new permanent amphitheatre and thereby win public approbation. In fact, the name the 'Colosseum' may derive from a gigantic statue of Nero which once stood in the vicinty.

The intensity of the Roman passion for combat, especially against wild beasts, forced the architects to resolve the problem of containing as many people as possible in the maximum possible safety. This aim resulted in the creation of the am-

24

24. MODEL OF THE COLOSSEUM (Museum of Roman Civilisation). Built by the Emperors Vespasian and Titus, it was opened in 80 AD and could accommodate 56,000 spectators who watched fights of wild beasts and gladiators.

25. THE COLOSSEUM. A masterpiece of Roman engineering skills, it was built of travertine, tufa and brick reinforced with concrete. During the Renaissance much of the stone was plundered for new buildings.

26

phitheatre (from the Greek word meaning 'double theatre'), the most characteristic achievement of Roman architecture, not least for its mastery of constructional techniques. The solution to the problem was based on technical advances made by the Romans during the preceding centuries, notably their revolutionary use of the arch and the vault, and their ingenious use of concrete and brick.

Nothing on this scale had ever been conceived before, and the incredible speed of its construction suggests that the unknown architect worked in a highly organized manner. It is known that different gangs of specialist workmen, each group using only one kind of stone (tufa, travertine, etc.) worked simultaneously on different sections of the building in order to finish it quickly. The site was well chosen: it was centrally placed in the city and had been previously occupied by the artificial lake of the Golden House of Nero, so that the ground was already excavated and well drained, and suitably strong foundations of travertine could be laid to support the exceptionally heavy weight of the new building.

The external dimensions of the amphitheatre, which is oval in form, measure 188 metres by 156 metres, with a total circumference of 527 metres. The full height is 57 metres. A travertine skeleton was constructed initially and the tufa, concrete and brickwork added later. The exterior is constructed entirely of blocks of travertine arranged in three superimposed tiers of arches in the three orders (Doric, Ionic, and Corinthian), surmounted by a tall attic storey with Corinthian pilasters supporting the entablature. Originally huge decorative gilt bronze shields, whose supports are still visible, were hung between the windows of this storey. The travertine blocks were held together by iron clamps, and their removal during the Middle Ages is the cause of the gaps now visible between the blocks. A complex system of corridors running around the inside of the walls allowed for the free circulation of the vast crowds, and also buttressed the weight of the building. The seating was entirely of marble up to the top of the third storey, and above that of wood in order to reduce the weight. Originally there were seventy four entrances: four had elaborately carved marble porticoes surmounted by statuary, the rest were plain. It is still possible to read the numbers of the entrances inscribed in Roman numerals.

The maximum capacity of the amphitheatre was 56,000; the spectators were seated in different sections according to rank. Among the most impressive attributes of the building was the *velarium*, a sort of temporary tent-roof that covered all or part of the building and protected the spectators from the rays of the sun. Sailors, who were permanently housed nearby, stretched the great canopy over a rib-structure whose 240 ribs met in the middle. The centre of the building was occupied by the arena, of which only the underground walls survive. They were built to house the wild beasts, which were easily let into the arena through a system of trapdoors operated by counterweights.

At the inauguration of the Colosseum in 80 AD, games and gladiatorial contests were organized which lasted for a hundred days and in which 5,000 wild beasts were killed. But actually it is the gladiators who have made the Colosseum's name. They were athletic and physically powerful slaves from all parts of the Empire, trained in special schools, and then

24

VS·VIC   ALVMNVSVIC   ID·EVS·   CALLIMORIVS
VS·VIC
MAZICINVS

SER   PENIIVS

30

SER   PENIVS

*27-32. ROMAN MOSAIC OF
GLADIATORS (3rd century AD,
Borghese Gallery). These mosaics show
fights between gladiators and wild beasts,
as well as between the gladiators
themselves. The best fighters are identified
by name.*

31

LICENIIOSVS   ASTACIVS   ASTACIVS   IACVLATOR
PVRPVREVS·ENTINVS~BACCIBVS
RODAN
ASTIVVS

32

25

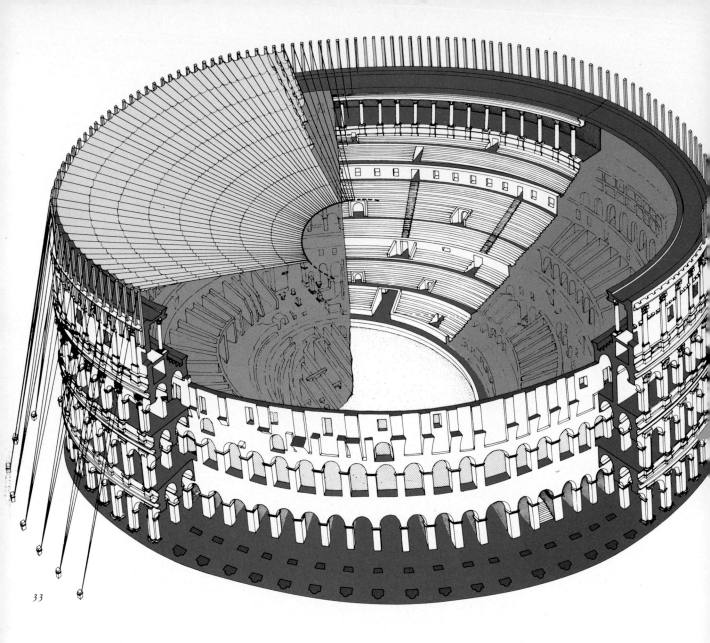

33

pitted against one another for the palm of victory. These barbaric contests ended in death for many of them, but the carnage has certainly been exaggerated. These men were highly trained entertainers, not easily replaced, and the Ancient Romans had enough commercial sense to get value for money from this precious commodity.

The Colosseum was later an ideal quarry for building materials, and only Benedict XIV's (1740-1758) consecration of the interior to the Passion of Christ saved it from further depredation. Unfortunately, by that time it had already been reduced to its present state of disrepair.

In its own day it was one of the wonders of the world, and since then it has stood as a symbol of the grandeur of Rome. For Henry James, it provided the setting for the poignant last scene in *Daisy Miller*, when his innocent young heroine catches malaria on a nocturnal visit to observe the great building by moonlight. And Byron translated the poem of the Venerable Bede (673-735):

While stands the Coliseum, Rome shall stand;
When falls the Coliseum, Rome shall fall;
And when Rome falls — the world.

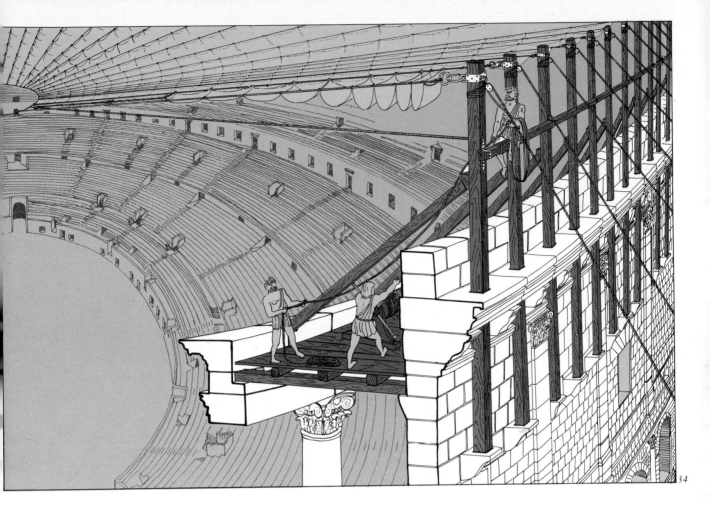

34

33-34. DESIGNS RECONSTRUCTING THE COLOSSEUM WITH THE
« VELARIUM ». *This enormous canvas sunshade was stretched across the
amphitheatre by sailors to protect the spectators from the sun.*

35. MODEL OF THE COLOSSEUM (*Museum of Roman Civilisation*).
*Originally there were 74 entrances; it is still possible to read some of the numbers
inscribed in Roman numerals over the entrance gates.*

36. RECONSTRUCTION OF THE UNDERGROUND GALLERIES OF
THE COLOSSEUM. *Note the complex system of trapdoors and cages via which the
beasts entered the arena.*

37. VIEW OF THE UNDERGROUND GALLERIES OF THE
COLOSSEUM. *The galleries, exposed by excavations, were originally covered by the
arena.*

35

36

37

THE PANTHEON

The Pantheon was built between 27 and 25 BC by Agrippa, son-in-law of Augustus, but its present appearance dates from the time of its restoration under Hadrian in the early 2nd century AD. The ensuing centuries have witnessed the refurbishment and embellishment of this magnificent building, which survives intact largely as a result of the Emperor Phocas' donation of it to the Christian community; at the instigation of Boniface IV it was made into a church in 609 AD. It was called St Mary of the Martyrs, because a vast quantity of relics of the martyrs were brought here from various catacombs. Restorations have maintained the building in such a good state of repair that the Pantheon remains the best preserved example of Roman architecture in existence.

The portico boasts sixteen monolithic Corinthian columns of

38

38. THE PANTHEON. Built in 27 BC by Agrippa, Augustus' son-in-law, it is
one of the best preserved temples of Ancient Rome.

39

Egyptian granite with marble capitals, 12.50 metres high and 1.50 metres in diameter. The bronze rafters on which the sloping roof rested were removed in 1632 by Urban VIII to be melted down and made into columns for the high altar of St Peter's, but happily the bronze door, the oldest of the three ancient Roman doors still in Rome, survived intact.

As soon as one enters the building, one is impressed by its monumental quality. Less expected, perhaps, is the perfect harmony of the interior, with the gentle curve of the dome floating above the uninterrupted expanse beneath. The geometry of cylinder and half-sphere is echoed by the simplicity of the dimensions, the height and diameter being identical. In antiquity the beautiful opening in the roof may have served the practical function of carrying off smoke and fumes from burnt offerings, but then as now its main purpose was to light the interior. The rain that it inevitably lets in is efficiently drained away through small holes in the floor. Worthy of note are the *Annunciation* attributed to Antoniazzo Romano (first chapel to right), and the statue of the *Madonna and Child* by Lorenzetto after Raphael (third pilaster to left), placed above the tomb of Raphael, who died on April 5th, 1520, at the age of thirty-seven.

39. THE DOME OF THE PANTHEON. *The coffered vault, originally gilded, surrounds the oculus, 8.40 metres in diameter, which lights the building.*

40. MODEL OF THE PANTHEON IN THE 2ND CENTURY AD *(Museum of Roman Civilisation). Originally the dome was covered with bronze tiles.*

41. TOMB OF RAPHAEL. *The artist was buried here after his death in 1520; the statue of the Madonna and Child by Lorenzetti was based on Raphael's design.*

42. VIEW OF THE INTERIOR. *The walls, 6 metres thick, are covered with red and yellow marble which gives some idea of the splendour of Imperial Roman architecture.*

43. Antoniazzo Romano (?), THE ANNUNCIATION. *A charming fresco of the 15th century.*

41

2

43

CASTEL SANT'ANGELO

An ancient Roman law prohibited the burial of anyone within the walls of the city, so that cemeteries and mausoleums could only be located outside. When the Emperor Hadrian decided to construct a great mausoleum for himself and his successors, he chose what was undoubtedly the most arresting site available on the right bank of the Tiber, near the Via Cornelia and visible from the *Campus Martius*, which had become one of the most important areas of Imperial Rome.

Construction began in 135 AD and was completed in 139 under Antoninus Pius. From an 80 metre square base, 15 metres high, there rose a cylinder 21 metres high and 64 metres in diameter. The upper part, topped by a cypress-covered mound, culminated in a colossal statue of Hadrian. At the same time as the construction of the mausoleum, it was decided to build a bridge to connect the tomb and the rest of the city directly. This bridge, now known as the **Ponte Sant'Angelo**, was originally called the *Pons Aelius* after the Emperor. The three central arches constitute one of the best pre-

served and most elegant Roman bridges in existence; the two outer arches were added in 1892 during the operations to regulate the flow of the Tiber.

Once it had been deprived of all its marble adornments and funerary associations, its situation and strategic importance as the link between the city and the Vatican made it natural to turn the mausoleum into a defensive post. Is is said that Pope Gregory the Great, during a procession to pray for the end of a plague then raging, saw the Archangel Michael sheathing his sword above the building. This signalled the end of the citizens' sufferings (590), and henceforth the mausoleum has been called the 'Castel Sant'Angelo'. During its history it has been used both as a fortress and as a prison, and owes the present appearance of its interior to the patronage of Popes Alexander VI and Julius II at the end of the 15th and beginning of the 16th centuries.

44. Gaspar van Wittel (1653-1736), CASTEL SANT'ANGELO AND ST PETER'S VIEWED FROM THE TIBER (Palazzo dei Conservatori). Painted by a Dutch artist who settled in Rome and painted many attractive views of the city.

45

47

34

45. *CASTEL SANT'ANGELO SEEN FROM THE PONTE SANT'ANGELO. The original bridge was built by Hadrian in 134 AD. It is now decorated with ten statues of angels by Bernini (completed in 1658) and, at the end nearest the castle, statues of Peter and Paul.*

46. *Pieter van Verschaffelt (1710-93), THE ANGEL. Traditionally Gregory the Great, while crossing the bridge to pray for an end to the plague that was raging, saw a vision of an angel sheathing a sword, whereupon the plague ceased.*

47. *MODEL OF THE MAUSOLEUM OF HADRIAN (Museum of Roman Civilisation). Castel Sant'Angelo was originally built as a mausoleum for Hadrian and his family in 139 AD. In the Middle Ages it was used as a citadel.*

48. *THE COURTYARD OF THE ANGEL. Named after the angel by Raffaele da Montelupo which originally crowned the castle. The cannon balls were part of the castle's munitions; the little Chapel of Leo X was designed by Michelangelo.*

49. *AERIAL VIEW OF CASTEL SANT'ANGELO. Situated on the banks of the Tiber, it was a natural citadel for the city in the Middle Ages.*

48

49

THE CAPITOL

The Capitol is one of the seven hills on which Rome was founded in the first half of the 8th century BC. From its position overlooking the most easily forded stretch of the Tiber, the Capitol has always been one of the most important areas of the city, both as a defensive refuge and as a commercial centre. Since the period of the Kings of Rome the hill had been regarded as a sacred place, but it was the construction of the Temple of Jupiter, Juno and Minerva at the start of the Republic, and the building of other temples dedicated to lesser divinities that made the Capitol into the religious centre of the Empire. Over the centuries all these magnificent classical buildings have suffered from the ravages of time, so that only ruined fragments survive. The great transformation of the Capitol took place in the first half of the 16th century, when the popes decided to make it the political centre of the city, and to take advantage of the fact that ancient memories of the glories of Imperial Rome gave the place a special prestige. Michelangelo was given the task of reorganizing and designing the whole area: his masterly solution is evident as we climb the grand steps, and even more so in the piazza itself, surrounded by impressive palaces and with the famous bronze statue of **Marcus Aurelius**, long believed to represent Constantine, at its centre. The **Palace of the Senators**, opposite the steps, with the statues of the goddess Roma and of the rivers Tiber and Nile, is now the seat of the municipal government of Rome.

The palaces on either side of the Palace of the Senators house the **Capitoline Museums**, founded in 1471 when Sixtus IV gave the Roman people a collection of bronzes which were exhibited in the Palazzo dei Conservatori. **The Capitoline Museum** was opened in 1871, and contains an important collection of classical sculpture, including the *Capitoline Venus*, the *Dying Gaul*, the *Laughing Silenus*, and a room of Roman portrait busts. In the **Palazzo dei Conservatori** are exhibited the *Lupa*, or she-wolf (Etruscan, 5th century BC), the famous *Spinario*, or boy pulling a thorn from his foot (1st century BC). There is also an interesting picture gallery.

50

50. MODEL OF THE CAPITOL AS IT APPEARED AT THE TIME OF THE EMPIRE (Museum of Roman Civilisation). Dominated by the Temple of Jupiter Capitolinus (dedicated in 509 BC) where the consuls took their vows on taking office, and where victorious generals gave thanks, it has always been the political centre of Rome.

51. PALACE OF THE SENATORS AND THE CAPITOL (*Piazza del Campidoglio*). Still the official seat of the governor of Rome, it was built over the ancient Tabularium (State Archives) in 1592 by della Porta and Rainaldi, on a design of Michelangelo's.

51

52. AERIAL VIEW OF THE CAPITOL. Situated on one of the seven hills of Rome, the square was designed by Michelangelo, although only completed in the 17th century. The bronze equestrian statue of Marcus Aurelius in the centre is one of the few to survive from antiquity.

52

53. EQUESTRIAN STATUE OF MARCUS AURELIUS. This statue, depicting the emperor-philosopher (161-180), is a masterpiece of Roman sculpture.

54. Pieter Paul Rubens (1577-1640), ROMULUS AND REMUS (Capitoline Pinacoteca). For the painting of this canvas Rubens was helped by other artists, however, the hand of this Flemish master is clearly apparent in this work.

55. Giovanni Bellini (c. 1426-1516), PORTRAIT OF A YOUNG MAN (Capitoline Pinacoteca). Some critics believe this work to be a self-portrait of the artist.

56. Caravaggio (1573-1610), SAINT JOHN THE BAPTIST (Capitoline Pinacoteca). The prophet is portrayed when a young man, carrying a newly-captured ram.

54

56

57

5

59

57. THEATRICAL MASKS (*mosaic 2nd century AD, Capitoline Museum*). *This mosaic, made up of minute fragments of coloured stone, depicts the masks of tragedy and comedy.*

58. BUST OF A ROMAN (*bronze, Capitoline Museum*). *This bust was originally believed to be a portrait of Brutus, Caesar's assasin.*

59. THE « SPINARIO » OR BOY PULLING A THORN FROM HIS FOOT (*Greek bronze, 1st century BC, Palazzo dei Conservatori*). *The boy is usually identified as Marcius, a Roman messanger who carried out his mission even though tortured by a thorn in his foot.*

60. THE DYING GALATIAN (*Roman copy of a Greek original, Capitoline Mueseum*). *A Celtic warrior wounded in battle.*

61. THE CAPITOLINE VENUS (*Capitoline Museum*). *A splendid Roman copy of a Greek original dating from the 3rd century BC, the goddess is about to take her bath.*

60

THE TIBER ISLAND

The small island in the Tiber, 300 metres by 80 metres, is the only island in the river and was dedicated to Esculapius, the god of healing. According to an old legend, the sacred serpent of Esculapius, which had been brought from Epidaurus in Greece, the centre of his cult, in order to protect Rome from a severe plague, fled and took refuge on the island as soon as the ship carrying it drew near. Consequently a temple was built in the god's honour (289 BC). The island is joined to the city by two very ancient Roman bridges. The one that links it with the left bank is the second oldest in existence after the Milvian Bridge (109 BC), and was built by Lucius Fabricius (*curator viarum*) in 62 BC. The other, which links the island with the district of Trastevere, is the Pons Cestius, built at the end of the 1st century AD by the consul Lucius Cestius.

62

62. MODEL OF THE THEATRE OF MARCELLUS (*Museum of Roman Civilisation*). *Showing it as it appeared in the 1st century AD with the Tiber Island in the background.*

63. THE THEATRE OF MARCELLUS. *This theatre, built by Augustus in the 11th century BC in memory of his grandson Claudius Marcellus, was transformed into a citadel in the 12th century and into a palace in the 15th century.*

64. THE TIBER ISLAND. *Dedicated to Esculapius, the god of healing, it is linked to the city by two Roman bridges of the 1st century BC.*

63

64

65

65. *SANTA MARIA IN COSMEDIN. Founded in the 6th century and rebuilt in the 8th and 9th centuries by Greek monks, it is one of the few Roman churches to preserve its 8th-century interior. Its seven-storied Romanesque bell-tower is very fine.*

66

66. *THE « BOCCA DELLA VERITÀ » (Santa Maria in Cosmedin). Originally the cover to a Roman drain, popular tradition claims that the mouth will bite off the hand of any perjurer.*

67

67. THE SYNAGOGUE. Designed by Osvaldo Armanni and Vincenzo Costa and built between 1874-1904. Situated near the Tiber in the centre of the old Ghetto, its architecture was inspired by that of ancient Assyria and Babylon.

68. THE SYNAGOGUE. View of the interior.

68

69. THE TEMPLE OF VESTA.
Roman temple of the 1st century AD, it was originally dedicated to the Victorious Hercules, and was erroneously called the Temple of Vesta because of its circular form.

70. THE TORTOISE FOUNTAIN (Piazza Mattei). Designed in 1584 by Giacomo della Porta; the four youths each hold a tortoise which drinks from the basin above.

PIAZZA NAVONA

Piazza Navona is undoubtedly the most attractive piazza in Rome, quite unlike any other in the city, or elsewhere. It is the centre of the quarter of the city known since antiquity as the *Campus Martius*, an area which marked one boundary of the city in the late Middle Ages. The name 'Navona' is said to derive from the *agones*, or contests, which took place in the Circus of Domitian here. During the Renaissance and Baroque reconstruction of Rome the Pamphili family built their own palace and other houses on the ruins of the circus, using them as foundations so that the piazza took on the shape and dimensions of the ancient stadium, (240 metres by 65 metres).

Beside the Palazzo Pamphili, commissioned by Innocent X (1644-1655), the same pope had the chruch of **Sant'Agnese in Agone** built on the spot where Saint Agnes was traditionally supposed to have been stripped for martyrdom, at which point the miraculous growth of her hair covered her shame. Most of the responsibility for this typically curving Baroque design was Borromini's, but his ideas proved too radical, and the church was completed in a more sober style by Carlo Rainaldi. The piazza contains three fountains which considerably enhance its impressive appearance. The two outer ones, the *Fountain of the Moor* and the *Fountain of Neptune*, are little more than accompaniments to the splendid focus of the piazza, Bernini's **Fountain of the Four Rivers**, with its statues of the Danube, the Ganges, the Nile, and the Plate, representing the four continents of the known world.

71. PIAZZA NAVONA. Built over the ruins of the ancient Circus of Domitian, it retains the shape of a race course. The Pamphili family financed the project in the 17th and 18th centuries, the Church of Sant'Agnese in Agone is by Borromini.

72

72. THE FOUNTAIN OF THE FOUR RIVERS. *Designed in 1651 by Gian Lorenzo Bernini, the four gigantic figures represent the Rivers of the Danube, Ganges, Nile and the Plate; the fountain is surmounted by an obelisk.*

73. THE SPANISH STEPS AND THE CHURCH OF TRINITÀ DEI MONTI. *The flight of 137 steps was built by Specchi and de Sanctis in 1721, flower sellers, students, and tourists gather here in the warm weather. The church and the 2nd-century AD obelisk dominate the view.*

74. THE FOUNTAIN OF THE SINKING BOAT *(Piazza di Spagna).* *Designed in 1629 by Pietro Bernini, the father of Gian Lorenzo Bernini, the boat appears to be sinking in a deep basin, water pouring from its poop and prow.*

75. THE TREVI FOUNTAIN. *Constructed in 1734 by Nicolò Salvi, this is the most famous fountain in Rome. Seventeen and a half million gallons of water pour through it each day. It is said that a traveller who throws a coin into the fountain will return to Rome.*

76. THE FOUNTAIN OF TREVI. *Detail.*

76

77. VIA VENETO BY NIGHT.
One of the most elegant and famous streets
of Rome, with many cafés and bars, it was
constructed at the beginning of this century.

78. THE FOUNTAIN OF THE
NAIADS (Piazza della Repubblica).
One of the largest and most successful
modern fountains of the city, it was built in
1888-1901 by Mario Rutelli and
Antonio Guerrieri.

79. THE TRITON FOUNTAIN
(Piazza Barberini). This beautiful
fountain of a triton blowing a jet of water
through a conch shell was designed in
1634 by Gian Lorenzo Bernini for
Urban VIII.

PIAZZA VENEZIA

This square is situated at the heart of Rome, where the most important roads converge. It is named after the **Palazzo Venezia**, on the west side of the square. Begun in 1455 for Paul II, this was the residence of the Venetian ambassador from the 16th century, and during the Fascist period, the seat of the government. Today it houses the Museum of Palazzo Venezia. Opposite the Corso is the grandiose **Monument to Vittorio Emmanuele II**, built between 1885 and 1911 to commemorate the Unification of Italy. It also contains the tomb of the unknown soldier.

80

81

80. MONUMENT TO VITTORIO EMANUELE II. This monument, designed by Giuseppe Sacconi, also contains the tomb of the unknown soldier.

81. PALAZZO VENEZIA. Built c. 1445 for the Venetian Cardinal Pietro Barbo, who later became Paul II (1464-71), today it houses the Museum of Palazzo Venezia.

82. MONUMENT TO VITTORIO EMANUELE. The first king of a United Italy is seen on his charger in the centre of the monument, built from 1885 to 1911 to commemorate the Unification of Italy.

SAN PIETRO IN VINCOLI

The basilica, one of the most ancient in Rome, was founded by the Empress Eudoxia, wife of Valentinian III, to house the chains (*vincoli*) which St Peter had worn in prison. It is now most famous as the location of Michelangelo's statue of *Moses*. This is the centrepiece of the tomb of Julius II, a pale shadow of the monument with over forty figures which Michelangelo had intended to make the central focus of St Peter's. The death of the pope in 1513 left Michelangelo without effective patronage, so that although he worked on for many years this work was left unfinished. The actual figure of *Moses*, carved between 1513 and 1516, remains a triumph of energy and in-tensity, clutching the tablets on which the Ten Command-ments were inscribed, and angry at the Children of Israel's profane adoration of the Golden Calf. The curious detail of his being represented with horns is the result of an error in the Latin translation of the Bible (Exodus XXXIV, 35). On either side stand the two very beautiful statues of *Leah* (hold-ing a wreath and a mirror) who represents active life, and *Ra-chel*, who stands for contemplative life. Michelangelo carved these figures in 1542-4, at the age of nearly seventy, and they are instilled with the more introspective quality of his later works.

85

83. *SAN PIETRO IN VINCOLI. Traditionally said to have been founded by the Empress Eudoxiana in 442 as a shrine for the chains St Peter wore in prison, the facade is by Meo del Caprina (1475).*

84. *THE SHRINE OF THE CHAINS OF ST PETER. The two chains with which St Peter was fettered when in the tullianum (a Roman dungeon).*

85. *MOSAIC OF SAINT SEBASTIAN. Probably dating from the 7th century, it is in a very good state of preservation.*

87

86. Michelangelo (1475-1564), MOSES. The awe-inspiring statue, carved between 1513-16 as a part of the tomb of Julius II planned for St Peter's, is now the centrepiece of a much smaller tomb erected here in the 1540's.

87. Michelangelo, MOSES. Detail of the head. The Prophet was at that date usually shown with horns due to a mistranslation of Exodus which said that Moses had « horns », rather than rays of light, around his head.

THE BORGHESE GALLERY

During the pontificate of his uncle Paul V (1605-1621), Cardinal Scipione Borghese decided to build a summer residence not too far from the city and from his official residence situated in the *Campus Martius*. The cardinal's favourite architect, Giovanni Vasanzio, (Jan van Xanten, of Dutch origin) was given the commission and built the villa. It stands in an immense and attractive park, which extends for many acres from the Porta Flaminia to beyond the Aurelian Wall. It took three years to complete (1613-1616), and was filled almost at once with a number of the fine art treasures that the Borghese family had collected from all over Italy. The villa was rebuilt in 1782 by Marcantonio Borghese, at which time it was decorated by Mariano Rossi, Gavin Hamilton, and others.

The collection of Roman statues, mosaics, and other antiquities was made up largely from objects discovered on the Borghese estates, but the main strength of the Gallery is its remarkable array of Renaissance and Baroque masterpieces. It possesses an especially fine collection of sculpture, starting with Canova's representation of *Pauline Borghese*, Napoleon's sister, as Venus Victorious (1805). There follows Bernini's *David*, a prodigious achievement, executed in 1619 when the young genius was only twenty-one years old. The *Apollo and Daphne*, its poignant story drawn from Ovid's *Metamorphoses*, is a slightly later proof of the sculptor's virtuosity, and there are further works of genius, the *Pluto and Proserpina* and the unfinished *Truth Unveiled by Time*.

The first floor contains the Picture Gallery. It has works by such masters of the Renaissance as Raphael (*Entombment, Lady with a Unicorn*), Correggio (*Danaë*), Giovanni Bellini (*Madonna and Child*), Antonello da Messina (*Portrait of a Man*), and several works by Titian, including *Sacred and Profane Love*, the supreme mythological picture of the great Venetian's early years. The Baroque is most notably represented by an unrivalled collection of works by Michelangelo Merisi, called Caravaggio. They include the *Boy with a Basket of Fruit*, the *Bacchus*, the *David*, and the *Madonna and Child with Saint Anne*.

88

88. *Antonio Canova (1757-1822), PAOLINA BORGHESE. The sister of Napoleon is represented as Venus Victorious. The statue dates back to 1805.*

89. *Antonello da Messina (c. 1430-79), PORTRAIT OF A MAN. One of the numerous portraits by this famous Sicilian artist who worked mainly in Venice.*

90. *Raphael, YOUNG WOMAN WITH A UNICORN. This portrait, attributed to Raphael, dates from the early 16th century. The unicorn symbolises chastity.*

89   *90*

91. *Sandro Botticelli (c. 1441-1506), MADONNA AND CHILD WITH ST JOHN AND ANGELS. Probably the work of pupils from Botticelli's workshop. The delicate colours and the sinuous forms are based on an original design by Botticelli.*

92. *Giovanni Bellini (c. 1430-1516), MADONNA AND CHILD. A signed work which reveals the delicacy and serenity of this Venetian master's later works.*

93. *Raphael (1483-1520), THE DEPOSITION. One of the first masterpieces by Raphael, painted in 1507 in memory of the son of a noble Perugian family.*

91

92   *93*

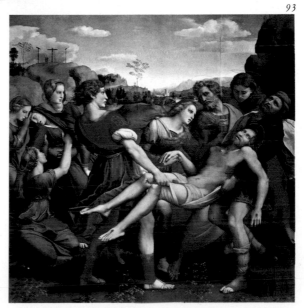

94

94. *Titian (c. 1487-1576), SACRED AND PROFANE LOVE. This early masterpiece by the Venetian master, painted for a wedding, is an allegory of the two aspects of love: spiritual and physical.*

95. *Dosso Dossi (1489-1542), THE ENCHANTRESS CIRCE. The Ferrarese artist portrays with rich allegory the enchantress described by Homer, while she awaits the arrival of Ulysses.*

96. *Vittore Carpaccio (c. 1465-1525), PORTRAIT OF A WOMAN. The woman's hairstyle identifies her as a woman of the court.*

97. *Lucas Cranach (1472-1553), VENUS AND CUPID. A carnal and mannered vision by this great master of the German Renaissance.*

98. *School of Leonardo (16th century), LEDA AND THE SWAN. This work represents Leda and Jupiter, transformed into a swan; from their union Castor and Pollux were born.*

99. *Pietro Longhi (1702-85), THE DANCE. A friend of Carlo Goldoni, Longhi excelled in portraying gracious, costumed scenes which document life in the 17th century.*

95

96

100. *Correggio (c. 1489-1554), DANAË. This painting portrays the legend of the nymph Danaë whom Jupiter tried to kidnap by transforming himself into golden rain.*

101. *Gian Lorenzo Bernini (1598-1680), DAVID. One of the first works by this artist (1619). David is captured during a moment of concentration before lancing the stone that will kill the giant Goliath.*

102. *Gian Lorenzo Bernini, THE ABDUCTION OF PROSERPINA. Pluto is portrayed in the act of abducting Proserpina; at the feet of the two figures lies Cerberus, the three-headed dog who guards the underworld.*

103. *Caravaggio, ST JOHN THE BAPTIST. The prophet is portrayed when a young man in the desert with a ram and a berry tree.*

104. Caravaggio (c. 1573-1619), BOY WITH A BASKET OF FRUIT (c. 1589). Caravaggio often masterly depicted baskets and compositions of fruit.

105. Gian Lorenzo Bernini, APOLLO AND DAPHNE. A masterpiece of baroque sculpture (1624). Daphne transforms herself into a laurel to escape Apollo.

106. Veronese (1528-88), THE SERMON OF THE BAPTIST. Even though unfinished, this work highlights Veronese's rich and sumptuous use of colour.

PIAZZA DEL POPOLO

This grandiose piazza, situated at the extreme north of the old city, takes its name from the small medieval church (9th century) built on the traditional site of Nero's tomb, over which grew a vigorous poplar (*populus* in Latin). The mis-translation of « *populus* » as « *popolo* » (people) gave the square its present name. Its proximity to the Porta Flaminia, where the 2nd century BC Via Flaminia linking Rome to the north began, meant that it was always a focal point of the city. It is the point of arrival for anyone coming from the north and is connected by three major roads to the religious (Vatican), political (Capitol), and tourist (Piazza di Spagna) centres of the city.

It was notably embellished by Sixtus V (1585-90) as part of his programme of urban improvement. He had the obelisk moved here from the Circus Maximus, where it had been placed by the Emperor Augustus. It is inscribed with hieroglyphics that date it to the period of Rameses II. In the 17th century, during the pontificate of Alexander VII, the twin churches of Santa Maria dei Miracoli and Santa Maria di Montesanto were built to designs by Bernini.

Santa Maria del Popolo, the little church built over Nero's tomb, was completely reconstructed in the 15th century. The first and third chapels on the right are frescoed by Pinturicchio (1485-9), who also painted the apse vault; the opulent second chapel belonged to the Cybo family and was designed by Carlo Fontana. The apse contains the splendid tombs of Cardinal Girolamo della Rovere and Cardinal Ascanio Sforza, both by Andrea Sansovino (c. 1505). The chapel to the left of the high altar holds two masterpieces by Caravaggio (c. 1569-1609): the *Crucifixion of St Peter*, and the *Conversion of St Paul*. The second chapel on the left is the magnificent Chigi chapel, designed by Raphael for the immensely rich Sienese banker Agostino Chigi (c. 1520). The altarpiece is by Sebastiano del Piombo, and two of the statues — the *Daniel* and the *Habakkuk* — are by Bernini.

107

107. PIAZZA DEL POPOLO VIEWED FROM THE PINCIO GARDENS.
Designed for Pius VII by Giuseppe Valadier in 1814, this square marks the convergence of many important roads, and was the entrance to the city in the days of the Grand Tour.

THE NATIONAL MUSEUM OF VILLA GIULIA

The Villa Giulia was designed for Julius III by Vignola and Ammannati in 1550-55. Vignola's stern facade gives no hint of the semi-circular portico of the garden front and the delightful *Nymphaeum* by Ammannati. This papal summer residence is set in a park which once stretched down to the Tiber. Since 1889 the Villa Giulia has housed the Museum of Etruscan and Italic Art, where archeological treasures of the pre-Roman period are beautifully displayed.

8

108. BRONZE HANDLE OF A CIST 4TH CENTURY BC. *The handle is composed of two warriors bearing the body of their dead comrade.*

109. APOLLO. *Etruscan terracotta found at Veii, early 5th century BC, one of a group of figures representing the fight between Apollo and Heracles for the Hind.*

110. TERRACOTTA SARCOPHAGUS OF A HUSBAND AND WIFE *(terracotta, 6th century BC). The couple are reclining on a couch and feasting. An exceptional example of Etruscan art, the hands and feet are particularly delicate.*

111. THE SCASATO APOLLO (Etruscan art, 2nd century BC). Discovered in the temple of Scasato, near Faleri, this bust shows the influence of classical Greek art.

1

112. THE FICORONI CIST (Etruscan bronze 330-300 BC). Discovered at Palestrina and engraved with motifs from Greek mythology, it was used to hold toiletries.

112

1

113. MALE PORTRAIT the so-called TESTA DEL MANGANELLO (1st century BC Etruscan Art). Discovered at Caere, a particularly realistic work which may be compared with those of Roman art.

MUSEO DELLE TERME

The museum is housed in the old Carthusian monastery of **Santa Maria degli Angeli**, whose church was adapted by Michelangelo from the Tepidarium (or warm pool) of the **Baths of Diocletian** (298-306 AD): other rooms of the Baths contain part of the museum. It was founded in 1889 and was intended to accommodate all Greek and Roman works of art and remains excavated within the city since 1870. The collection was particularly enhanced in 1901 by the acquisition of the exceptionally fine Ludovisi Collection.

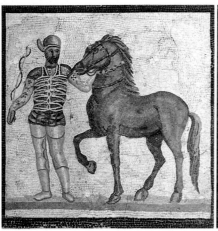 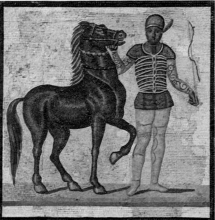 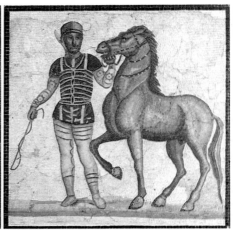

114-116. ROMAN MOSAICS OF CHARIOT HORSES AND THEIR GROOMS. The rival stables are distinguished by the different racing colours of the grooms.

117. THE LUDOVISI THRONE. The Birth of Aphrodite. Greek original of the 5th century BC. One of the most beautiful surviving Greek reliefs, it formed the back of a throne for a cult goddess.

117

65

9

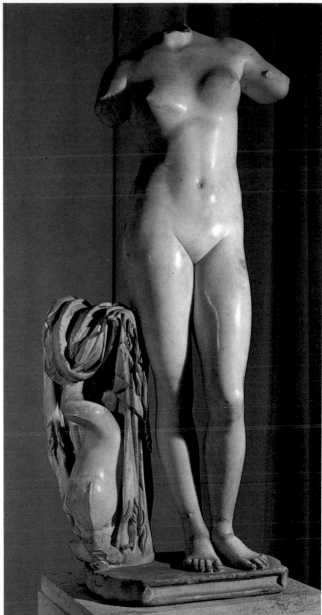

120

21

118. THE LANCELOTTI DISCOBOLOS. *Roman copy of a Greek bronze by Myron, this is the best preserved and most complete copy of the Olympic discus thrower.*

119. NIOBID. *Roman copy of a Greek statue of the 4th century BC. It represents one of Niobe's daughters who has been shot in the back with an arrow by Apollo.*

120. VENUS OF CYRENE. *Original Greek work of the 4th century BC showing the goddess just risen from the sea; a dolphin supports her robe.*

121. BOXER. *A bronze of the 2nd century BC, signed by Apollonius. The exhausted boxer sits resting after his fight.*

Two large lateral chapels were added later to give the church a Latin Cross plan. That on the right was built by Sixtus V (1585-90) as a family mortuary chapel and also to commemorate the sainted pope, Pius V, who is buried in the tomb on the left of the entrance. The left-hand chapel is called the Pauline or Borghese Chapel after its patron, Paul V (1605-21). It is richly adorned with precious marbles, frescoes, and monuments, and is indicative of the opulent taste of the period. The altar, decorated with agate and lapis lazuli, incorporates an ancient image of the Virgin, traditionally said to have been painted by St Luke; above it is a bronze bas-relief depicting the *Miracle of the Snow*, with Pope Liberius tracing the plan of the basilica.

128

128. *APSE MOSAIC OF THE CORONATION OF THE VIRGIN. Made for Nicholas IV by Jacopo Torriti in 1295, it includes portraits of the pope on the left and Cardinal Colonna on the right, beneath are scenes from the Life of the Virgin.*

SAN PAOLO FUORI LE MURA

Towards the end of the 1st century AD a small funerary chapel was built over the tomb of St Paul; it survived intact until the age of Constantine. Shortly after the official recognition of Christianity a small church was constructed on the site and consecrated in 324 by Pope Sylvester I, but it proved too small to accommodate the multitude of pilgrims who flocked to the tomb of the apostle. In 395 the Emperor Theodosius decided to build a much larger basilica, which was completed under the Emperor Honorius and was richly decorated with artistic treasures over the ensuing centuries.

Theodosius' splendid basilica survived the Barbarian invasions and the ravages of time, but in 1823 it was almost completely destroyed by a fire that started in its wooden roof. Marble monuments, paintings, mosaics, and other irreplaceable works of art perished in the disaster; only the apse mosaic, Arnolfo di Cambio's *baldacchino*, and Galla Placidia's mosaic on the grand triumphal arch survived.

The reconstruction of San Paolo fuori le Mura (St Paul's without the Walls) was begun immediately, financed by contributions sent from all over the world, and the basilica was consecrated by Pius IX in 1854. Fortunately the architect Luigi Poletti resisted any temptation to alter the original design. Many years later, in 1928, Calderini's portico was added to the facade, and the imposing statue of St Paul by Canonica placed at its centre.

On entering the basilica one is not merely impressed by the sheer size of the building — it is 127 metres long — but also by the simplicity of its architectural language. Four rows of columns divide the central nave and paired aisles, while the soft light derives from the alabaster decorations of the windows. Above the columns are mosaic portraits of all the popes. The cloister to the right of the basilica, attributed to Vassalletto (13th century), is one of the supreme masterpieces of the Cosmatesque style of decoration in Rome.

129. *SAN PAOLO FUORI LE MURA. The largest church in Rome after St Peter's, the present basilica was rebuilt after a disastrous fire destroyed the ancient church in 1823.*

130. THE CLOISTER. *Originally part of the old Benedictine convent it was finished before 1214. The coupled colonnettes, decorated with mosaic, have small animals crouching between the columns.*

131. *APSE MOSAIC OF CHRIST ENTHRONED BETWEEN THE FOUR EVANGELISTS. Above are the Elders of the Apocalypse with St Peter and St Paul. Originally made in the 13th century, they have been much restored.*

130

131

ST JOHN LATERAN

The basilica of St John Lateran, which was built by Pope Sylvester I in 324 on the site of the ancient property of Plautius Lateranus, is the Cathedral of Rome, with the pope as its bishop. It is consequently the Mother and Head of all the churches of the city and of the Catholic world. Like so many other churches in Rome, it was originally dedicated to Our Saviour, and like St Paul's, it is has suffered destruction by sacking, fire, and earthquake, but has always been reconstructed.

Its main facade is one of the most impressive achievements of the Roman 18th century, and the most notable work of Alessandro Galilei (1734). The *atrium* has five doors, the farthest to the right being the Holy Door, opened only in Jubilee Year, while the middle portal has doors of bronze originally made for the Curia, transferred here by order of Alexander VII.

The interior was completely remade in the second half of the 17th century by Borromini. He remodelled the Early Christian interior, then in a state of collapse, and created a harmonious and cool Baroque effect that successfully incorporated the ornate 16th-century roof. The niches on either side of the fine central space of the nave are populated by statues of the apostles after Bernini, and above them there are reliefs by Algardi of scenes from the Old and New Testaments. In front of the 14th-century Gothic canopy over the Papal Altar, the *Confessio* contains the tomb of Martin V, an early Renaissance work by Simone Ghini. In 1884 Leo XIII paid for the reconstruction of the apse and the Papal Throne, or *cattedra*. Above is the much restored mosaic, originally executed by Jacopo Torriti at the end of the 13th century. It represents *Christ with the Virgin and Saints* flanking the jewelled cross. The smaller figures of St Francis and St Anthony of Padua are included because the church was administered by the Franciscan Order. The basilica is flanked by an attractive 13th-century Cosmatesque cloister.

132

132. ST JOHN LATERAN. The cathedral of Rome, the facade dates from the 18th century and was designed by Galilei. The extreme right-hand door is the Holy Door, only opened in Holy Years. The Monument to St Francis of Assisi is by Giuseppe Tonnini (1927).

133

134

133. *VIEW OF THE NAVE. In the 17th century Borromini gave the nave its dramatic appearence by adding the niches in the piers which house the gigantic statues of the Twelve Apostles by pupils of Bernini.*

134. THE HOLY STAIRS. *Believed to be the staircase from Pilate's house which Christ descended after his condemnation, brought to Rome from Constantinople by St Helena. The devout ascend the steps on their knees.*

74

THE CATACOMBS

Legend speaks of the catacombs, a dense network of underground galleries extending beyond the ancient urban circle of Rome, as shelters where the first Christians might have gathered to escape persecution. In fact the catacombs were used almost exclusively as burial grounds and the digging of the galleries, sometimes on as many as five superimposed levels, arose out of the necessity to exploit to the utmost the limited amount of land belonging to the wealthier Christians; the price of land in Rome was in fact very high and the number of Christians continually growing.

It was the conformation of the subsoil, containing many underground tunnels previously built for plumbing purposes, and the burial rite, which had replaced cremation, which were to determine the lay-out and the width of the galleries.

Studded with loculi, often closed by slabs of painted or sculpted marble, or with small cells known as cubicles, the walls of which were sometimes painted, the catacombs were used as cemeteries until the 5th century.

Having been the burial grounds of saints and marytrs the catacombs became, during the Middle Ages, the destination of many pilgrimages. At the beginning of the 9th century the reliquaries of numerous saints and martyrs were transferred to churches then being built within the walls of the city. Thus the catacombs were slowly abandoned and their entrances, overgrown with vegetation or hidden by landslides, disappeared. Their systematic rediscovery began in the 16th century and the catacombs today are among the most fascinating and frequently visited sights of ancient Rome.

135. THE PAPAL CRYPT (the Catacombs of Calixtus). These catacombs, named after Pope Calixtus (217-222), became the official burial place for the bishops of Rome.

136. THE CATACOMB OF THE GOOD SHEPHERD (the Catacombs of Domitilla). This 2nd-century catacomb contains the earliest known representation of Christ as the Good Shepherd.

137

137. THE *CATACOMBS OF CALIXTUS*. *Crypt with frescoes of saints and flowers.*

138. INTERIOR OF THE MAUSOLEUM OF ST CONSTANCE. *The mausoleum is part of the monumental complex of Sant' Agnese in Agone.*

139. THE *CATACOMBS OF PRISCILLA*. *View of the Greek Chapel or the Room of the* Fractio Panis.

139

140. THE GOOD SHEPHERD (*the Catacombs of Priscilla*). *Detail.*

141. THE TOMB OF CECILIA METELLA ON THE APPIAN WAY. *The wife of Crassus, one of Caesar's generals; this tomb was transformed into a fortress in the 13th century to defend the city.*

142. THE STONE OF « DOMINE QUO VADIS? » ON THE APPIAN WAY. *According to holy legend the imprint of Christ's feet was left in this stone when He appeared to St Peter who was fleeing from Rome.*

143. THE APPIAN WAY. *The oldest Roman road, constructed by Appius Claudius in the 4th century BC to link Rome to Brindisi.*

141

143

77

VATICAN CITY

The State of the Vatican City was created by the signing of the Lateran Treaty on February 11th, 1929. The city covers an area of 109 acres and has about 1,000 inhabitants. Bernini's colonnade around **St Peter's Square** determines its boundary to the east, while the wall around the Vatican Gardens marks its other frontier. This minute state, the smallest in existence, which is officially acknowledged by almost all the nations of the world, has its sovereign the Supreme Pontiff, the Pope, who, in accordance with the same treaty, also extends his authority over certain other important buildings on Italian soil — notably the Lateran Basilica and the Lateran Palace, Santa Maria Maggiore, San Paolo fuori le Mura, the Catacombs, and a number of palaces which enjoy extraterritorial rights, including the pope's summer residence at Castel Gandolfo. As a sovereign state, the Vatican is entitled to run its own postal service, to mint its own coin which is valid tender throughout Italy, to sign treaties, and to maintain diplomatic relations. Police services and ceremonial duties are performed by the Swiss Guard, who wear a magnificent orange and blue uniform, said traditionally to have been designed by Michelangelo. The Swiss Guard were chosen by Julius II in 1506 to be his personal bodyguard after they had proved themselves particularly brave in battle. Three other bodies of guards, created in the 19th century, were abolished by Paul VI in 1970; they were the Palatine Guard, the Noble Guard, and the Papal Gendarmerie.

The Vatican State is dominated by the enormous **Basilica of St Peter's** and its Square, which in part cover the ancient Vatican Hill from which the State takes its name. To the north of the basilica are the **Vatican Palaces**, a great sequence of buildings constructed over the centuries after the return of the papacy from its exile in Avignon in 1377. At

144. *THE HOLY DOOR OF ST PETER'S. The door on the extreme right of the facade of the basilica is only opened by the pope in Holy Years, for the rest of the time it remains bricked up.*

145. *ENTRANCE TO THE VATICAN PALACE. On duty at the entrance is a member of the Swiss Guard, the personal bodyguard of the pope, founded in 1506 by Julius II.*

146. THE FACADE AND THE
FOUNTAINS. *The fountain to the right
was designed by Carlo Maderno (1614),
the second was added in 1667.*

that time the old Lateran Palace, which had been the official papal residence since the age of Constantine, was found to be in a state of total decay, and the pope moved to the Vatican. Nicholas V (1447-55) transformed the old house standing by St Peter's into a palace built around a courtyard (the *Cortile del Pappagallo*). The **Sistine Chapel** was added by Sixtus IV in 1473, and the **Belvedere** on the Vatican hill by Innocent VIII in the 1480's. Alexander VI, the Spanish pope, built a suite of rooms (the **Borgia Apartments**) which were colourfully frescoed by Pinturicchio, but these rooms proved to be too cramped for Julius II who, at the beginning of the 16th century, moved up a floor and had his rooms decorated by Raphael (**Raphael Stanze**). Later popes added the Library and a series of museums, the latest of which is the **Museo Storico** built in 1973 by Paul VI.

Although in the 16th century the popes ruled large areas of the country around Rome (the Papal States), over the centuries these territories diminished in size and the power of the papacy dwindled. What had once been a European force became merely a national one. Apart from the basilica and the palace, the rest of the Vatican is occupied by the famous gardens lying on the highest part of the hill. Tree-lined avenues, fountains, and little grottoes make the Vatican Gardens an oasis of calm, a refuge for the pope in his free moments.

The pope is Bishop of Rome and, as successor to the first bishop, St Peter, the head of the Roman Catholic Church. He enjoys supreme jurisdictional power over the whole church in which he is assisted by the Roman Curia and the Sacred College of Cardinals. In 1962 the number of cardinals in this body was increased to eighty-seven. The Roman Curia consists of twelve Sacred Congregations who cope with the administration of the Church, three Tribunals, and six Offices.

It is the duty of the College of Cardinals to elect the new pope. On the death of a pope they go into Conclave (Latin, meaning a locked room) in the Sistine Chapel, the entrance to which is then double-locked. The cardinals meet twice daily before voting and scrutinizing the votes. If the outcome of the vote is negative then black smoke issues from the chimney of the Sistine Chapel; if a new pope has been elected the smoke is white. The name of the new pope is then proclaimed from the central balcony of St Peter's.

The only freely accessible parts of the Vatican are the Square and Basilica, and the Vatican Museums.

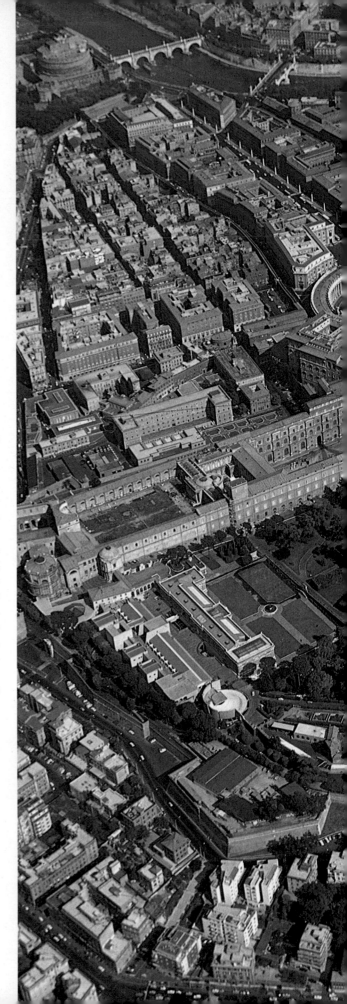

147. AERIAL VIEW OF ST PETER'S BASILICA AND THE VATICAN CITY. The great colonnade of Bernini marks one boundary of the tiny Vatican State, and the walls surrounding the Vatican gardens are another.

148

82

148. *VIEW OF ST PETER'S SQUARE BY NIGHT.*

149. *VIEW OF ST PETER'S SQUARE. Bernini's colonnade encircles this vast area, whose centre is marked by the obelisk which once stood in Caligula's Circus.*

THE BASILICA OF ST PETER'S

The most recent archaeological excavations under the basilica leave no room for doubt of the existence of the tomb of the Apostle Peter directly under the high altar.

In 324, only a few years after the Edict of Milan (313 AD), the construction of a monumental basilica dedicated to St Peter began on the very spot on which he had been buried after his martyrdom. This first basilica, about half the size of the present St Peter's, was a very magnificent version of the Early Christian basilica. Preceded by a large colonnaded *atrium*, or courtyard, the wide nave was flanked by pairs of aisles, and at the east end there was a broad transept and a curved apse. The basilica was vaulted by a pitched wooden roof, and during the Middle Ages a splendid array of works of art and monuments was added. During the 15th century, when it was apparent that the building was falling into disrepair, several popes attempted to restore St Peter's. But it was only Julius II who decided on a total reconstruction (he was also thinking of a suitably magnificent setting for his gigantic tomb, which was already being designed by Michelangelo, but which ended in San Pietro in Vincoli). Bramante started on the demolition work with such enthusiasm that he won himself the epithet « *Bramante rovinante* » (Bramante the ruiner). In 1506 the foundation stone for the new basilica was laid; the plan was Greek Cross (i.e. with all four arms of the cross of

150

150. *THE BLESSING OF THE POPE IN ST PETER'S SQUARE. On solemn occasions a crowd of pilgrims unite in St Peter's square to receive the blessing « Urbi et Orbi » which the pope imparts from the loggia of the basilica.*

151. THE INTERIOR OF ST PETER'S. *The largest basilica in the Christian world. The nave measures 193 metres long and 44 metres high. The transept is 140 metres long.*

the same length), but in 1514 both pope and architect were dead. In the years that followed first Raphael, then Giuliano da Sangallo, and later Peruzzi worked on the design, alternating between Greek Cross and Latin Cross plans. In 1548 Paul III entrusted the completion of the work to Michelangelo, and to him we owe the design of much of the east end, as well as the great cupola (partly inspired by the dome of the cathedral of his native Florence). Michelangelo went to supervise the work almost daily, riding on a mule. On his death in 1564 Giacomo della Porta completed the dome, and finally in 1605 Paul V instructed Carlo Maderno to elongate the nave into a Latin Cross and build the facade and portico (1607-12). In the centre of the facade is the **Benediction Loggia** from which each newly-elected pope gives the blessing *Urbi et Orbi* (addressed to the city and the world).

The interior of the basilica gives an impression of genuine grandeur, as well as overwhelming the visitor with its vast scale. Standing by the third pier of the nave it is possible to appreciate the fine balance between its immense length and enormous height. Whereas the lines of the plan have a Renaissance clarity, the decoration is entirely Baroque, and this disparity illustrates just how greatly attitudes and conceptions of beauty changed in the hundred years or more it took to complete the project. Bernini designed the monumental *baldacchino* (1624-33) at the crossing for Urban VIII, using bronze taken from the Pantheon and melted down. He also designed the *cattedra*, or Chair of St Peter, as well as one of the colossal saints (*Longinus*) in the niches of the crossing piers — all arresting works of art. Also to be seen is Arnolfo di Cambio's venerable bronze statue of *St Peter* (13th century) and, of a rather later date, mosaic copies of the altarpieces that once adorned the basilica. Of all these treasures, however, Michelangelo's *Pietà* is the most precious (first chapel on the right). He carved it in 1499-1500 at the age of twenty-three, and it is his only signed work. The tenderness of Mary's grief as she cradles the dead Saviour on her knees cannot fail to move, and the softness and humanity of the sculpture remains an everlasting miracle.

St Peter's Square, designed by Bernini and built between 1656-67, is elliptical in form; it is surrounded by a colonnade of 284 Doric columns, four deep, surmounted by 140 statues of Holy Martyrs by Bernini's shool. In the centre stands a great obelisk, made from a single block of granite 25 metres high, which was transferred here from the Circus of Nero by order of Sixtus V in 1585. It was the first obelisk to be moved in the modern era and the work, supervised by Domenico Fontana, took four months, with 900 workmen and 140 horses helping to get it into place.

152. VIEW OF THE INTERIOR OF THE CUPOLA. In the pendentives are gigantic mosaics of the Four Evangelists; the whole dome is diffused with light.

153. THE NICHE OF THE PALLIUMS. *Situated under the papal altar, above the tomb of St Peter; it is here that the palliums were consecrated for the newly-elected bishops.*

154. THE PAPAL ALTAR AND THE BALDACHIN OF BERNINI. *The bronze used for this baldachin was taken from the dome of the Pantheon.*

153

153. THE NICHE OF THE PALLIUMS. *Situated under the papal altar, above the tomb of St Peter; it is here that the palliums were consecrated for the newly-elected bishops.*

154. THE PAPAL ALTAR AND THE BALDACHIN OF BERNINI. *The bronze used for this baldachin was taken from the dome of the Pantheon.*

155

155. ST PETER ENTHRONED. *The bronze statue of the first pope, shown blessing and holding the keys of Paradise, was probably made in the 13th century; it is attributed to Arnolfo di Cambio.*

156. THE CATTEDRA. *Made by Gian Lorenzo Bernini of gilt bronze for Alexander VII in 1656-65, it encloses what is believed to be the original throne of St Peter. The statues are of the Four Doctors of the Church.*

157. Michelangelo, THE PIETÀ. *Carved when Michelangelo was twenty-five it is the only work to bear his signature, inscribed on the fillet across the Virgin's breast.*

158. Michelangelo, THE PIETÀ. *Detail of the Virgin's head. The Virgin Mary is represented as a young girl, her grief is expressed through the poignant gesture of one hand.*

159. Michelangelo, THE PIETÀ. *Detail of the hand of Christ.*

158

159

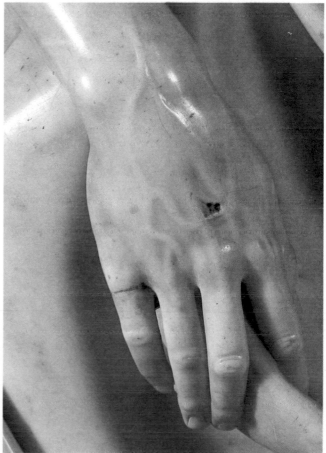

The Vatican Museums are unique both for the interest of their enormously diverse contents and for the buildings in which the collections are housed. The majority of the buildings in this vast complex were not designed to fulfil their present function, and this is particularly true of the part nearest to the basilica: the **Sistine Chapel**, the **Loggias** and the **Raphael Stanze**, the **Borgia Apartments**, and the **Chapel of Nicholas V** which originally formed part of the papal private residence.

To reach the museums we climb the monumental double staircase designed by Giuseppe Momo in 1932; it has independent ascending and descending ramps, and the bronze balustrade is decorated with the coats-of-arms of the popes. There is also a lift. It is not possible to visit all the various Vatican Museums in a single day. **The Pio-Clementine Museum**, created by Popes Clement XIV and Pius VI, is housed in the **Palazzetto del Belvedere**, a late 15th-century building. It contains an impressive collection of classical sculpture found during excavations on papal territory, and was significantly enlarged in the early 19th century by Pius VII in part of the complex of rooms linking the Belvedere with the papal residence. The **Etruscan** and **Egyptian Museums** are also here (Gregory XVI, 1836). In order to reach the Sistine Chapel and the Raphael Stanze, we pass through the **Gallery of the Candelabra**, the **Gallery of the Tapestries**, and the **Gallery of the Maps**. Near the entrance is the **Pinacoteca**, a marvellous collection of Renaissance and Baroque pictures, as well as the **Gregorian Profane Museum** and the **Pio-Christian Museum** (moved here from the Lateran in 1970), and the **Missionary-Ethnological Museum**.

160

160. MONUMENTAL STAIR-
CASE AT THE ENTRANCE TO
THE VATICAN MUSEUMS.
*Designed in the 1930's by Giuseppe
Momo, this double-ramped staircase
is decorated with papal
coats-of-arms.*

161. SISTINE SALON (Apostolic
Library). *Built in 1588 by Domenico
Fontana on Sixtus V's request. The walls
were decorated by various artists, directed
by Cesare Nebbia, with episodes from the
papacy of Sixtus V.*

162. THE GALLERY OF MAPS.
*Decorated for Gregory XIII by Ignazio
Danti, the walls are painted with maps
and plans of Italy and of papal territory
at Avignon (1580-83).*

161

162

95

163

164

163. THE BIGA (Room of the Biga).
A two-horse carriage reconstructed from
antique fragments by Francesco Franzoni
in 1788. The original « biga » probably
dated from the 1st century AD.

164. LACOON (Pio-Clementine
Museum). This group, made c. 50 BC
by sculptors from Rhodes was dug up in
Rome in 1506. The High Priest of Troy
and his sons were crushed to death by a
snake.

165

165. *SALA ROTONDA (Pio-Clementine Museum). Modelled on the Pantheon, the room contains a vast porphyry vase from Nero's Golden House, and antique statues.*

166. *THE ALDOBRANDINI MARRIAGE (Apostolic Library). A rare masterpiece of Augustan art (1st century BC), it was found on the Esquiline in 1605 and depicts a marriage scene.*

166

167. *THE AUGUSTUS OF PRIMA
PORTA (Braccio Nuovo). The Emperor
Augustus (27 BC-14 AD) is shown
raising his hand, about to deliver a speech.*

168. *THE BELVEDERE
APOLLO (Pio-Clementine Museum).
Roman copy of a Greek original in bronze
dating from the 4th century BC. One
of the finest representations of the
Apollonian divinity.*

169. *THE « DOGMATIC »
SARCOPHAGUS (Pio-Christian
Museum). Made for a married couple
who are portrayed in the centre,
surrounded by scenes from the Old and
New Testament.*

170. *Giotto (1266-1337), THE
STEFANESCHI ALTARPIECE
(Pinacoteca). Once on the High Altar of
Old St Peter's, this double-sided panel
shows Christ Enthroned on one side, St
Peter on the other.*

171. *Carlo Crivelli (1430-1494),
THE PIETÀ (Pinacoteca). The
anguished despair expressed in this
paintinig is typical of this Venetian
painter.*

167

168

169

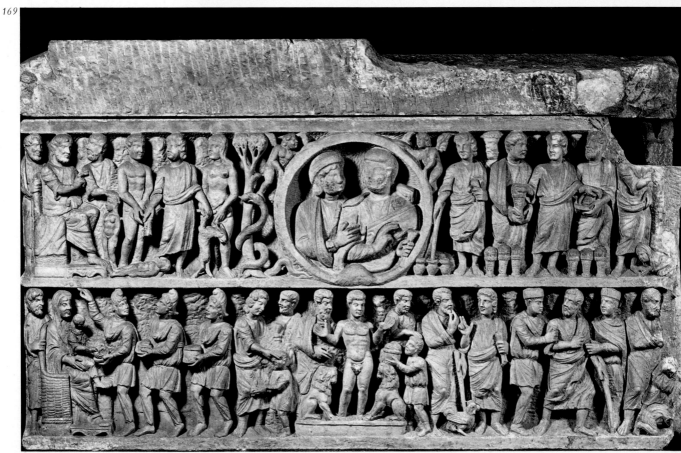

170

99

172

173

172, 173. *Melozzo da Forlì (1438-94), TWO MUSICIAN ANGELS (Pinacoteca). These fresco fragments once formed part of the decoration of the church of Santissimi Apostoli.*

175. *Leonardo da Vinci (1452-1519), ST JEROME (Pinacoteca). This unfinished panel painting expresses the anguish of the penitent saint, beating his breast, while the lion's roar echoes his grief.*

174. *Fra Angelico (1401-55), SCENES FROM THE LIFE OF ST NICHOLAS OF BARI, DETAIL (Pinacoteca). A typical, lyrical narrative painting by the Florentine Dominican monk.*

174

176. *Raphael (1493-1520), THE TRANSFIGURATION (Pinacoteca). One of the last works painted by Raphael.*

177. *Caravaggio (c. 1573-1610), THE DEPOSITION (Pinacoteca). A masterpiece of expressive realism, the pattern of the hands of the mourners lead down to the heavy body of the dead Christ.*

Nicholas V (1447-55) began to build the new papal residence on a site between Old St Peter's and today's Belvedere Courtyard, which at that time had yet to be built. For him Fra Angelico painted the beautiful Chapel of Nicholas, with *Scenes from the Lives of St Stephen and St Lawrence*. Successive popes added to the residence; the Borgia pope, Alexander VI, had a suite of rooms on the first floor decorated by Pinturicchio, but his successor, Julius II, found these rooms too cramped and moved to the floor above. Here there was a series of four rooms which had been decorated in the 15th century by great artists including Piero della Francesca; but Julius, who had already begun to demolish Old St Peter's, was never worried by destruction. The old decoration was swept away, and a twenty-five-year-old artist from Urbino, Raphael Sanzio, was entrusted with the commission to paint the papal apartment — possibly on the recommendation of the pope's architect, Bramante, who also came from Urbino. These four rooms are now universally recognized as some of the greatest decorative schemes of all time.

178. THE DISPUTE OVER THE HOLY SACRAMENT (Stanza della Segnatura). Probably the first fresco Raphael painted, it represents the affirmation of the dogma of Transubstantiation.

Room of the Fire in the Borgo (1514-17)

This room, the third to be painted, was started after the death of Julius II, and glorifies his successor, Leo X, for whom it served as a dining room. The pope chose scenes from the lives of his illustrious predecessors Leo III (795-816) and Leo IV (847-55) and had himself portrayed as both of them. The first scene to be painted was the *Fire in the Borgo*, which is probably entirely by Raphael. It represents an incident which occurred in 847: fire broke out in the Borgo of St Peter's, but was extinguished when Leo IV made the sign of the Cross. The Pope is shown in the background, giving his blessing from the balcony of Old St Peter's, while the foreground is filled with figures desperately attempting to quench the flames. The muscular male nudes show the influence of Michelangelo, but the woman balancing a waterjug on her head on the extreme right is one of Raphael's most beautiful inventions. The other frescoes in this room are clumsily painted and are probably the work of Francesco Penni and Giulio Romano, who worked from Raphael's designs without really understanding them. On the right is the *Coronation of Charlemagne by Leo III*, which took place on Christmas Day 800; next comes the *Oath of Leo III*, also set in Old St Peter's; and the final scene is the *Victory of Leo IV over the Saracens at Ostia* (849) which refers to the Crusade against the Turks that Leo X had recently proclaimed. Behind the pope is a portrait of Cardinal Giulio dei Medici, Leo's nephew, who was later to become Clement VII. The 15th-century groined vault is still preserved, painted with the *Glorificatoin of the Trinity* by Perugino.

Room of the Segnatura (1508-11)

This room was the first to the painted by Raphael for Julius II. It was intended to house the pope's small private library (bookcases were arranged along the walls beneath the frescoes, but were later removed) and the subject matter of the paintings, presumably worked out by scholars in consultation with the pope himself, is appropriately humanistic. In roundels on the vault are personifications of *Theology*, *Poetry*, *Philosophy*, and *Justice*. As we enter, we see on the opposite wall the *School of Athens*, representing the triumph of philosophy. Set against a magnificent temple-like building (inspired possibly by Bramante's plans for the New St Peter's or, more probably, by classical architecture) is an assembly of the greatest philophers and scientists of antiquity. In the centre on the left stands Plato, pointing to the heavens and carrying a copy of his book *Timaeus* (it has been suggested that this is a portrait of Leonardo); by his side is Aristotle, pointing to the earth

179. THE MASS AT BOLSENA (Room of Heliodorus). Illustrates a miracle which took place in 1263. The pope who commissioned the painting, Julius II, is portrayed kneeling before the altar.

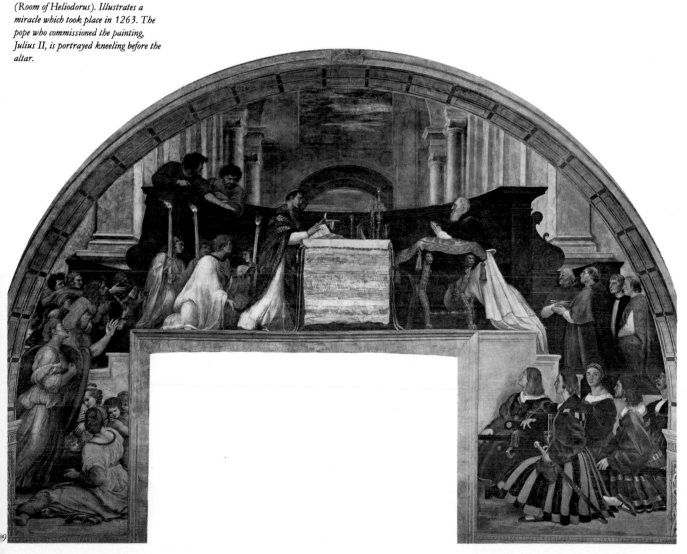

and holding his book *Ethics*. Other figures are recognizable: Socrates, with his protuberant forehead, stands to the left of the central pair, disputing with his audience; in the right-hand foreground Euclid demonstrates a theorem to his pupils, using compasses and a slate; on the left Epicurus, with a crown of vine-leaves, props his book against the base of a column, and Pythagoras, dressed in pink and white, writes in a book while a youth holds a slate before him inscribed with his theory of harmony. The bearded man in the centre foreground leaning against a block of marble represents Heraclitus (a portrait of Michelangelo); the old man lying slouched on the steps is taken to be Diogenes, and on the extreme right Raphael included his own self-portrait in a black cap; nearby is Zoroaster, holding a sphere.

On the opposite wall is the *Dispute over the Holy Sacrament*, in which the mysteries of the Transubstantiation and of the Holy Trinity are debated both in heaven and on earth. The Trinity is the central focus of the composition; God the Father appears above the *mandorla* surrounding God the Son, and the Holy Ghost hovers over the altar of the sacrament. Seated in the clouds are figures from the Old and New Testaments including (from the left) St Peter, Adam, David with his harp, and on the right, amongst others, St Paul, Abraham, and Moses. On earth, the Fathers of the Church and early popes glorify the Trinity.

To the right of the Dispute is the *Parnassus*, the mountain of Apollo and the nine Muses, a scene which celebrates the triumph of poetry. Using the window embrasure to create the mountain, Raphael arranges the most famous ancient and modern poets according to their themes: the lyric poets, tragedians, epic poets, etc. In the centre Apollo strikes up on his viol, the muses draped around him; on the left blind Homer dictates to a seated youth, and Dante's severe profile can be seen behind. In the left foreground, the serpentine figure of Sappho is particularly beautiful.

The lunette of the last wall shows the three cardinal virtues of *Prudence*, *Temperance*, *Fortitude*, and *Justice*, who sits enthroned above them. On either side of the window are *Gregory IX Approving the Decretals*, the pope being a portrait of Julius II, and the *Emperor Justinian Receiving the Pandects*, which allude respectively to Ecclesiastic and Civic Law.

Room of Heliodorus (1512-14)

This room, painted immediately after the Room of the Segnatura, shows a significant advance in Raphael's powers both as a dramatist and as an illusionist; his compositions are more ambitious and his colours richer. The room was intended to be the audience chamber of Julius II, whose portrait appears prominently in the Heliodorus and Bolsena scenes. After Julius' death in 1513, however, the new pope, Leo X, had his

180. MOUNT PARNASSUS (Stanza della Segnatura). Painted for Julius II between 1508-11, the scene represents Poetry and shows Apollo with the nine Muses and famous poets of all ages.

portrait inserted in the Attila fresco. The theme of the room remained the same: divine intervention in the life of men, combined with Julius' desire to rid Italy of foreign invaders.

The room is named after the fresco of the *Expulsion of Heliodorus from the Temple*. Raphael illustrated a highly dramatic scene from the second Book of Macabees concerning a Syrian, Heliodorus, who attempted to loot the Temple of Jerusalem. The High Priest, who is seen in the centre distance, prayed for divine help, and a heavenly horseman appeared and drove the interloper from the temple. Julius II, carried in a litter, witnesses the scene from the left-hand side.

The scene to the right depicts the *Miracle at Bolsena*. A Bohemian priest who doubted the presence of Christ in the Eucharist, was celebrating mass at Bolsena, when the Host bled at the moment of consecration (1263). Orvieto Cathedral was built to hold the relic of the Holy Corporal, and the incident is commemorated by the feast of *Corpus Domini*. Pope Julius is shown kneeling before the altar at which the miracle occurs, attended by cardinals and his personal body-guard, the Swiss Guards.

On the opposite wall Raphael's virtuosity reaches new heights in the *Liberation of St Peter from Prison*. The natural light from the window below makes the surrounding wall dark, and Raphael illuminates it with the pale moon, veiled by cloud, the flare of the soldier's torch, and the supernatural light emanating from the angel, who first wakes the slumbering St Peter and then leads him to freedom. Pope Julius was titular cardinal of the church of San Pietro in Vincoli, hence the choice of subject.

The final scene is the *Repulse of Attila from the Gates of Rome*. A preliminary drawing shows that Raphael originally intended to give the pope Julius II's features, but substituted Leo X on his accession. Leo the Great had defended Italy from Attila the Hun with the divine intervention of Saints Peter and Paul; the event took place on the banks of the River Mincio, but in the fresco Rome is seen in the background. This scene refers to the Battle of Ravenna (11th April, 1512), at which Leo was present as a cardinal, when the French were expelled from Italy.

Hall of Constantine (1517-24)

After Raphael's sudden death in 1520 at the age of thirty-seven, his pupils Giulio Romano and Francesco Penni were entrusted with the completion of the project. Raphael had made some sketches for the large scene of the *Victory of Constantine over Maxentius*, but the other compositions are mostly the work of his successors. They represent: the *Vision of the Cross, Constantine's Baptism in the Lateran*, and *Constantine's Donation of Rome to Pope Sylvester in Old St Peter's*.

181. THE LIBERATION OF ST PETER (Room of Heliodorus). This dramatic night scene, lit only by the soldiers' flares and the supernatural light of the angel is one of Raphael's masterpieces.

182

182. THE SCHOOL OF ATHENS
(*Stanza della Segnatura*). *This work
represents Philosophy; next to Plato and
Aristotle are the great minds of antiquity.*

108

THE SISTINE CHAPEL

The Sistine Chapel was built between 1475 and 1481 by Pope Sixtus IV, from whom it takes its name. It was probably paid for by the money collected from pilgrims during the Jubilee Year of 1475. It formed part of the rebuilding programme through which the popes of the late 15th century hoped to re-establish Rome not only as the centre of Christendom, but also as the artistic capital of Italy, an aspiration which was finally realized in the early years of the 16th century.

It was necessary to build a suitably magnificent chapel in which the pope could celebrate mass before the cardinals and a select lay audience. The old Vatican Chapel built by Nicholas III (1277-81) had been destroyed, and the very beautiful chapel decorated by Fra Angelico for Nicholas V (1447-55) was too small for such gatherings. Consequently the architect, Giovanni de' Dolci, was instructed to build, after the project formulated by Baccio Pontelli, an extremely plain vaulted structure, lit by six windows on each side, specifically for mural decoration. A Cosmatesque pavement was laid down, a *cantoria*, or choir stall, was set into one wall, and a screen, decorated with Sixtus' coat-of-arms was placed across the chapel (it was later moved towards the entrance wall in order to enlarge the presbytery). This screen was probably designed by Mino da Fiesole. The floor is on three levels: the highest, nearest the altar, has a projection on the left to accommodate the papal throne; the next level, between the altar and the screen, originally contained seating for the cardinals (although distinguished visitors with the right connections, such as Erasmus of Rotterdam, also obtained seats here); and, the area behind the screen was reserved for the laity.

The vault was painted blue, to represent the heavens, and gilded wooden stars were attached to it (all this was swept away some twenty-five years later when Michelangelo painted the ceiling). Sixtus then summoned the most famous Tuscan and Umbrian painters of the day to fresco the walls. The decoration was based on Early Christian programmes such as those formerly in Old St Peter's, with a frieze of full length portraits of the first canonized popes, starting over the altar with Christ at the centre and running between the windows. Below these are scenes from the *Life of Moses* (on the left wall)

and the *Life of Christ* (on the right), and lower still are fictive painted tapestries. Later the Medici pope, Leo X, was to commission Raphael to design tapestries which were hung over the painted ones on festivals; these tapestries are now in the Vatican Picture Gallery, and the designs, or cartoons, for them are in the Victoria & Albert Museum, London. Two of the original frescoes were lost when Michelangelo painted his great fresco of the *Last Judgement* on the altar wall, and the two scenes at the entrance are completely repainted. These frescoes, with their lavish use of gold and brilliant colouring, and their inclusion of contemporary portraits and Roman landmarks (the Arch of Constantine is visible in Botticelli's *Punishment of Korah, Dathan, and Abiram*) are all delightful narrative scenes, and some — especially those by Signorelli, Botticelli and Perugino — are masterpieces of 15th-century art. Starting from the altar wall they represent:

LEFT WALL
1. Moses in Egypt, and the Circumcision of his Son (Perugino)
2. The Burning Bush, and Moses Meeting the Daughters of Jethro (Botticelli)
3. The Crossing of the Red Sea (Cosimo Rosselli)
4. Moses on Mount Sinai, and the Worship of the Golden Calf (Rosselli)
5. The Punishment of Korah, Dathan, and Abiram (Botticelli)
6. Moses Giving his Rod to Joshua, and the Mourning over the Body of Moses (Signorelli)

RIGHT WALL
1. The Baptism of Christ (Perugino)
2. The Purification of the Leper, and the Temptation of Christ (Botticelli)
3. The Calling of Saints Peter and Andrew (Ghirlandaio)
4. The Sermon on the Mount and the Healing of the Leper (Rosselli)
5. The Donation of the Keys to St Peter (Perugino)
6. The Last Supper (Rosselli)

183. THE SISTINE CHAPEL. General view. Michelangelo's monumental fresco of the Last Judgement dominates this 15th-century chapel built by Sixtus IV.

184. Botticelli, THE PUNISHMENT OF KORAH, DATHAN AND ABIRAM (left wall). Painted between 1481 and 1483 the frescoes on this wall illustrate episodes from the life of Moses.

185. Perugino, THE DONATION OF THE KEYS TO ST PETER. One of the most beautiful 15th-century frescoes. St Peter, the first pope, is authorized by Christ to continue his mission on earth.

184

185

THE SISTINE CEILING

Pope Julius II (1503-13) was the nephew of Sixtus IV and consequently regarded the Sistine Chapel with family pride. After he had instigated the rebuilding of St Peter's, his thoughts turned to the chapel, and he summoned Michelangelo from Florence to paint the ceiling. Michelangelo was most reluctant to accept the commission (he complained in a sonnet of the extreme discomfort of working on a high scaffold, and protested that he was in any case not a painter). He had already undertaken the work on Julius' monumental tomb and would have preferred to continue with that project. However, from May 1508 until October 1512 he laboured on the ceiling, covering 540 square metres with paint and earning 6,000 ducats. When the ceiling was eventually unveiled to the public it caused a sensation.

The Sistine ceiling is probably the most complex and grandiose decorative scheme in Western art. The iconographic programme chosen by Julius was highly sophisticated (it is possible that Michelangelo was involved in the choice of subject matter himself) and the final design for the ceiling was equally elaborate. Given that he had to include such a variety of characters and biblical scenes, Michelangelo constructed an architectural framework into which all these various elements could be inserted. In order to link the curved vault to the walls below he painted vast thrones in the pendentives, on which are seated the Hebrew prophets and the pagan sybils who foretold the coming of the Messiah. In the spandrels and lunettes flanking the thrones are shown the *Ancestors of Christ*: sombre, frightened figures, living in a nether world before the

186

186. *Ghirlandaio, THE CALLING OF SAINTS PETER AND ANDREW (right wall). The frescoes on this wall illustrate episodes from the life of Christ.*

187. *Michelangelo, THE SISTINE CEILING. Painted with scenes from the Creation, the Fall of Man, the Forebears of Christ, and with the prophets and sybils who foretold His coming, Michelangelo worked on it from 1508-12.*

advent of the Lord. These men and women are remarkable feats of imagination, highly individualized although they are based solely on the list of names of Christ's forebears in the Gospel of St Matthew. In the four corner spandrels are prefigurations of salvation (*David and Goliath* and *Judith and Holofernes*) and of the Passion of Christ (the *Death of Haman* and *Moses and the Brazen Serpent*), and along the centre of the vault are depictions of the *Creation of the World*, the *Fall of Man*, and *Life after the Fall*. These scenes are surrounded by the *Ignudi*, naked youths personifying perfect corporeal and spiritual beauty who hold bronze medallions painted with mystical scenes from the Maccabean Histories. Yet despite this dense amount of subject matter, Michelangelo managed to preserve a sense of air and space by allowing the painted « sky » to show through at each end of the vault, particularly near *Zachariah* and *Jonah*.

The nine scenes from Genesis are painted so as to be read from the entrance; the sequence begins over the altar (alth-

ough in fact this end of the ceiling was the second half to be painted). The first scene, above the figure of *Jonah*, is the *Separation of Light from Darkness*, in which the violent, generative figure of God almost dissolves into the elements He is creating. Next comes the *Creation of the Sun, Moon and Plants*, in which God appears twice, while in the third scene, the *Separation of Land from Water*, He appears in a more benign mood. There follows the most famous fresco of the whole series, the *Creation of Adam*. The beautiful, languid figure of Adam, like some ancient river god, lies passively waiting for the vital spark of life to be transmitted to him from the Creator, who arrives in a clamorous throng of *putti* with the timorous Eve by His side.

The *Creation of Eve* takes place on some bleak, deserted shore; she is drawn from the side of the slumbering Adam by the terrible force of God's command. The next scene shows two consecutive events within one framework: the *Temptation*, and the *Expulsion from Paradise*. The composition is ingenious, the

188, 189. THE CREATION OF MAN. The most famous painting in the Sistine Chapel. God infuses life into the languid figure of Adam.

190. THE CREATION OF THE SUN, MOON AND PLANTS (detail).

191. THE CREATION OF WOMAN (detail). God commands Eve to come forth from the rib of the sleeping Adam.

192. THE FLOOD (detail). The tempest rages and desperate men and women attempt in vain to escape the flood.

Tree of Knowledge separates the two episodes and the contrast between the ease of Adam and Eve in the verdant, leafy Paradise and their despair in the bleak plain of the World is all too apparent. The last three scenes depict the tribulations and sorrows that beset Man after the Fall: the *Flood*, the *Sacrifice of Noah*, and the *Drunkeness of Noah*. This end of the ceiling was the first to be painted; the scaffolding was moved to the other end of the chapel early in 1511, by which time Michelangelo's treatment of the painting became freer and richer: this is apparent in the larger scale of the prophets and sibyls, starting with *Daniel* and the *Persian Sibyl*. By the time he painted *Jonah* over the altar wall the change in style is complete: the rich colour and violent movement of this figure (a prefiguration of Christ's death and resurrection, since Jonah spent three days in the belly of the whale before being thrown onto dry land) make it one of the most remarkable creations in the chapel.

190

191

193

194

196

195

118

193. THE DELPHIC SYBIL.

194. THE LYBIAN SYBIL.

195, 196. IGNUDI. *Male nudes, personifying perfect corporeal and spiritual beauty and grace.*

197. THE PROPHET ZACHARIAH *(detail).*

198. THE PROPHET JOEL *(detail).*

197

198

199. THE TEMPTATION AND FALL OF MAN. *This great double scene, separated by the tree of knowledge, contains the blissful life in Paradise and the wretched existence of Adam and Eve after the Fall.*

119

THE LAST JUDGEMENT

Enormous political and religious changes had occurred in Rome between the time of the decoration of the ceiling and the painting of the *Last Judgement*. For a century Rome had enjoyed a relatively stable relationship with the rest of Europe, but now two dramatic events changed the whole situation. The Protestant Reformation, and the Sack of Rome by the mercenary troops of the Holy Roman Emperor Charles V in 1527, shook Italy and seriously undermined the power of the papacy. In 1534 Paul III was elected pope, and it was he who initiated the serious internal reform of the Catholic Church which came to be known as the Counter Reformation. He was also one of Michelangelo's greatest patrons, and during his reign Michelangelo became architect of St Peter's as well as painting both the *Last Judgement* and the Pauline Chapel (which is still the pope's private chapel).

Once again, Michelangelo was loth to undertake the commission of the *Last Judgement*; he was now nearly sixty, and the physical energy required to execute a fresco of over 350 square metres with a composition containing more than 300 figures was very great. Michelangelo worked on the fresco from 1534 to 1541, and the painting was unveiled on All Hallows Eve of that year.

In the lunettes at the top of the wall, two groups of angels carry the symbols of Christ's Passion; those on the left have the Cross, those on the right bear the Column of the Flagellation. Lower down, in the centre, is the figure of Christ the Judge — not the compassionate Jesus of forgiveness and love, but an awesome and vengeful God from whom even His mother, the Virgin Mary, appears to shrink with fear, and on whom the supplication of St Peter has little effect. The action

200

200. THE LAST JUDGEMENT (detail). Christ as Judge; the Virgin Mary at his side, and below St Lawrence with his grid-iron and St Bartholomew with his flayed skin.

201. THE LAST JUDGEMENT. Painted between 1534 an 1541, twenty years after he had completed the ceiling, this is a terrifying and awesome vision of the Day of Judgement.

of Christ, raising His hand to strike down the damned, creates a whirlwind movement throughout the whole composition: the damned plummet headlong into hell on the right, and righteous spirits are borne up effortlessly to Heaven on the left, while the angels rush to obey the command of Christ, poised at the centre like the eye of the storm. Around Him are gathered the Elect: St Lawrence with the instrument of his martyrdom, the grid-iron; St Bartholomew holding up his own flayed skin, on which there is a distorted self-portrait of Michelangelo; St Catherine with her wheel; and, to the right, St Sebastian contemplating the arrows of his torment, and St Andrew holding his cross. Below the elect, a group of angels sound the Last Trump, calling humanity to Judgement. On the right a group of the damned implore mercy, but are violently repulsed, and Charon, the ferryman of the dead, whips them out of his boat with his into the gates of Hell. Here, Minos, the judge of the underworld, with a serpent entwined around his belly, watches over his company of sinners. Michelangelo gave him the features of his enemy, Biagio da Cesena, the Papal Master of Ceremonies who objected to the nudity of the figures. In the lower left-hand corner we witness the Res-

urrection of the Flesh as skeletons merge from the ground and are clothed with their heavenly bodies.

As Condivi, Michelangelo's pupil and biographer, wrote: "In this work Michelangelo expressed all that the human figure is capable of in the art of painting, not leaving out any pose or action whatever." Originally the figures were nude, but a later pope insisted in the interests of decency that draperies should be added, thereby earning the unfortunate artist, Daniele da Volterra, who undertook the work, the epithet « Braghettone » (literally the *breeches maker*).

The work is disturbing at first sight, and should remain so. Michelangelo's intention was not to please, but rather to instil sensations of fear and awe with this vision of the *Dies Irae*, and portray Man's struggle and suffering to attain Eternal Life.

202. THE LAST JUDGEMENT (detail). The boat of Charon which ferried damned souls over the River of Death to Hell.

TIVOLI

Twenty kilometres east of Rome, the city of Tivoli, formerly called Tibur, was probably founded by the Sicilians in the 10th century BC. In 380 BC the city was conquered by Roman troops led by Furio Camillo and from that moment on Tivoli became one of the most important fortified towns in the entire area. During the imperial era the wealthy Roman patricians transformed Tivoli into a resort. Sumptuous villas were built by Sallust, Cassius, Catullus, Horace and Maecenas; but undoubtedly the most grandiose of all was that built by the Emperor Hadrian (117-139 AD) of which imposing ruins still remain.

During the Middle Ages the town was once again fortified, and in 1460 Pope Pius II had a large castle built there.

Today Tivoli is one of the most interesting tourist attractions in the province of Rome. Apart from some important recently-discovered archaeological remains, it also numbers, among its other attractions, the monumental ruins of Hadrian's Villa and the gardens of the Villa d'Este.

Hadrian's Villa

This imposing residence, built by the Emperor Hadrian, is a unique example in the history of architecture because of the extent and the very original conception of the numerous buildings which go to make up this complex. Hadrian who began the building of the villa around 125 AD on his return from one of his numerous trips to the Orient, wanted to reproduce, over a large area of more than 150 hectares, all those buildings which he found artistically pleasing. Thus the most disparate architectural styles, developed according to differing conceptions and tastes, were brought together for the building of this imperial residence. Even though the proportions may differ from those of the originals such buildings as the **Lyceum**, the **Academy** and the **Pecile** of Athens — with their perfect classical lines — were skilfully reproduced and interspersed with other buildings such as the **Can-**

203. THE MARITIME THEATRE (Hadrian's Villa). A delightful nymph stands in the centre of this small island surrounded by a canal and a building.

204. THE CANOPUS (Hadrian's Villa). The name of this building, constructed around a canal dug into a small valley, recalls the Egyptian city of Canopus, renowned for its luxurious palaces overlooking a canal.

205. MODEL OF HADRIAN'S VILLA (Museum of Roman Civilisation). In the foreground stands the large building of the Pecile, and in the background the Imperial Palace; on the left the Greek Theatre and on the right the Thermal Baths, the Canopus and the Academy.

3

204

205

opus of the Nile delta near Alexandria in Egypt and the **Valley of Tempe** in Thessaly.

By far the most extraordinary innovation introduced into the building of this complex was the use of great quantities of water, canalized from the river Aniene, which together with the statues, mosaics, stuccoes and polychrome marbles, constitute one of the principal decorative motifs of this whole complex.

After Hadrian's death the villa was used only rarely by his successors and the lack of any exhaustive historical documentation means that no definite interpretation may be given to the various buildings which go to make up the villa.

Villa d'Este

Originally a Benedictine monastery, transformed in the 13th century into the Palace of the Governor of Tivoli, Villa d'Este owes its present appearance to Cardinal Ippolito d'Este, the second son of Alfonso d'Este, Duke of Ferrara and Lucrezia Borgia. Following his nomination as Governor of the city in 1550, Cardinal Ippolito decided to transform the ancient building into a sumptuous, princely residence. With the help of the architect and humanist Pirro Ligorio, he created a splendid park laid out on various levels. Using the water from the river Aniene, available in large quantities, Ligorio, with much imagination and skill, created the numerous fountains and plays of water which have made Villa d'Este famous throughout the world. Ligorio employed a system similar to that used by the Romans in Hadrian's Villa (a system exploiting the momentum of the water). He had an artificial underground canal built to convey the water from the river into the higher part of the garden; with an intricate system of canals, the water could then be distributed to the various levels of the park and, by simply exploiting the force of gravity, Ligorio was able to create jets of water of various shapes and sizes.

206. AVENUE OF A HUNDRED FOUNTAINS (Villa d'Este). Water rises from numerous fountains portraying, eagles, ships, lilies and obelisks.

208. THE FISHPONDS (Villa d'Este). In the background one can glimpse the splendid waterfall and the Fountain of the Hydraulic Organ.

207. THE ROMETTA FOUNTAIN (Villa d'Este). This work is intended as an allegory of Rome, with the statue of the wolf and twins representing the city and lower down in the basin a ship which represents the Tiber Island.

209. THE OWL FOUNTAIN (Villa d'Este). This fountain once had a very complex hydraulic system which caused an owl and various bronze birds to sing.

206

207

OSTIA ANTICA

A commercial centre of primary importance during the imperial era, Ostia today has become an archaeological centre of extraordinary importance. Ostia Antica in fact documents the urban, technical and social evolution of the whole of Roman history.

According to an ancient legend, Ostia was founded by Ancus Martius during the era of the Kings and developed notably under the republic, particularly in the 4th century BC when the first fortification of the *castrum* (the military encampment) was built. Already a famous port during the reign of Augustus, Ostia was transformed by the Emperor Claudius (37-41 AD) into an artificial sea-port by the building of the off-shore dyke on which stood the Lighthouse. Notably enlarged by the Emperor Trajan, with the construction of a large artificial lake on the mainland, Ostia became, in the centuries that followed, the most important commercial centre in the Mediterranean. The remains of the Commercial Centre, the **Theatre**, the **Forum**, the **Springs**, the **Public Baths**, the *Insulae*, the *Termopolia*, the shops and the temples belonging to the various religious communities, are all of great importance. A cosmopolitan city, Ostia boasts not only the *Mithraeum* (the sanctuary of the god Mithra) but also the remains of one of the most ancient synagogues.

210. THE THEATRE. Behind the proscenium which has been rebuilt, lies the Square of the Guilds; the Temple of Cerere marks its centre.

211. AERIAL VIEW OF THE EXCAVATIONS AT OSTIA. This antique city was once an important commercial centre at the mouth of the Tiber. From the 4th century onwards the fall of the town began, the population decreased and many buildings were ruined and buried. The excavation work which led to the rediscovery of the city only began in the 19th century and is still continuing.

210

211

INDEX OF MONUMENTS AND ARTISTS